Searching for Sully
Our stories

Ann Shaw

Searching For Sully - Our Stories
by
Ann Shaw

Copyright © Ann Shaw 2017

The right of Ann Shaw to be identified as the author of this work has been asserted by her in accordance with the Copyright, Design and Patents Act 1988.

All rights reserved. No part of this publication may be reproduced, stored in a retrievable system, or transmitted, in any form, or by any means, without the prior permission of the author.

ISBN 978-178456-467-4

Typeset in Minion Pro 12pt on 15.

Published and printed in Great Britain
by printondemand-worldwide.com

Contents

Acknowledgements
Preface
Brief history of Sully 1
Introduction - About Sully 3

PART 1
Inside Sully - memoir of a teenager
1 Searching for Sully 7
2 Patient number 07313 12
3 Lisa and Megan 17
4 Quick medical diagnosis 22
5 Corpse material 27
6 The assault 29
7 My new social life 33
8 TB patients over-sexed 37
9 Smoking, food and flowers 41
10 To cut or not to cut? 45
11 Ghosts in the machine 47
12 Settling in 50
13 Nessie, the "party woman" 54
14 Arrival of Mrs McGrath 59
15 Murder in Tiger Bay 64
16 Television and fresh air 67
17 Mistaken identity 72
18 Lisa leaves 78
19 An "Old hand" returns 80
20 The silk dresses 85
21 Negative and positive 88
22 Mrs McGrath - slippers and sex 92

23 "Do-it-yourself" gastrics	97
24 Love in Sully	99
25 The rotten apple	103
26 Jennifer and the vicar	105
27 Mrs McGrath discovers God	108
28 Bartering	111
29 Celebratory food	115
30 It's foolish but it is fun	118
31 Hospital rules and practical jokes	120
32 The Royal wedding	125
33 The woman who doesn't want to go home	128
34 Art in Sully	133
35 Welsh social class system	135
36 A marriage made in Sully	139
37 Matrimony and morals	144
38 Dentists and babies	149
39 Home to die	152
40 Departure of Big Mags	155
41 A visit from the Bible society	159
42 Bombshell	161
43 The mysterious boyfriend	164
44 The deed is done	168
45 Turning point	172
46 Death and departure	177
Epilogue: Pinewood Student Rehabilitation centre, Wokingham, Berkshire	181

PART TWO - Patients and staff stories
1930s 185
STAFF-NURSES:
Clara Gould: OBE first matron of Sully 185
Iris Deli: Most were terminal cases 188
1940s 190
STAFF-DOCTORS:
Dr Len West: Science is measurement 190
1950s 193
Coronation issue of Flotsam the hospital magazine 194
POEMS 195
PATIENTS' STORIES:
Joyce Jones: I found a wreath on my chest 205
Alan Workman: TB and heart patients strictly
forbidden to mix 208
Tony Hooper: It would have made a great resort hotel .. 209
Philip Cox: How they kept children in bed 210
Margaret Smith – experimental heart surgery 210
RELATIVES' STORIES:
Bernie Watts: Seeking family history 212
Peggy Horton – lived in a wooden shed 213
STAFF:
Pam Stephen: worked as a clerk 215
Dr. Bill Foreman: Superintendent Sully hospital 216
1960s 222
Hugh Thorp: trained in Sully – professor in Canada 222
STAFF - MEDICAL TECHNICIAN'S STORIES:
Steve Dorkings: Terrific camaraderie 223
PATIENTS' STORIES:
Stephen Parry: Most children died 225
Jenny Hicks: Still dream of the place 226

David Roberts: Regular trips to the Sully Arms 226
1970s 228
PATIENTS' STORIES:
Warren Lewis: I still have my poster from Sully 228
Ceri Williams (nee Pritchard): Happy Days! 230
Howard Richard: Only chance of survival 231
STAFF - NURSES:
Vivienne Griffin: Feeding the babies 232
Janet Phillips: Now living in Australia 232
STAFF:
Adrian Pike: International reputation for heart surgery . 236
1980s 238
STAFF:
Steve Parker: Party time in the nurses' home 242
Wayne Spencer: Great community spirit 242
1990s 246
PATIENTS' STORIES:
Tony Blackwell: Hot meals delivered from Bristol 244

Postscript 247

Searching for Sully ~ Ann Shaw

To my late mother, Marianne Rumsey,
who believed in me and never missed visiting
throughout my four years in Craig-y-nos
and later in Sully hospital.

Acknowledgements

I would like to thank all the former patients and staff
who have contributed to this book.
Without their stories this project
would not have been possible.

Also special thanks to the following
for their advice and assistance:
Malcolm Shaw, Mary Randall, Chris Holme,
Laura Fyfe, Jane Foreman and Hilary McRobbie

Disclaimer

Names have been changed to protect the privacy of individuals.

I have tried to recreate events and conversations based on my diaries and memories of them.

Brief history of Sully

Memory is like buried treasures. Sometimes you discover long forgotten worlds. So it is with my Sully diary written in 1960 and put away in a suitcase and forgotten about for decades.

Here I chronicled life inside Sully, an Art Deco building on the coast near Cardiff, a state-of-the art hospital designed to offer a more humane way of treating those with TB, in contrast to the traditional harsh regimes of sanatoriums based on isolation, and fresh air.

So it was with Sully, a part of my buried childhood past, kept locked away for more than half a century.

What would I find when I opened that suitcase? Ghosts that should be allowed to rest? Instead I found stories of humour, bravery, fortitude, stoicism, a whole colourful spectrum of social life encapsulating a period of social history never written about before. Yes, there were plenty of medical books on the fight against TB but little or nothing from the patient's perspective and certainly nothing from a child's or teenager.

For the past thirty years of my life I earned my living as a journalist. It was other people's stories I spent my days telling. In the end the itch to do something creative for myself won. I took redundancy and enrolled at Glasgow School of Art as a mature student for a degree in Fine Art, though secretly I wanted to write. My years in journalism had earned me a comfortable living and a pleasant lifestyle.

But in the back of my mind lingered my Welsh heritage, of stories waiting to be told.

Today, with the advance of technology, and the use of blogs, e-books and print-on-demand, we are all storytellers.

Introduction ~ About Sully Hospital (1936-2001)

Sully was a hospital, not a sanatorium, and was the last of several institutions and clinics to be established for the provision, treatment and abolition of TB by the King Edward V11 National Memorial Association and it was disbanded after the National Health Service came into effect in 1948.

The President of the Association and chairman of the Sully Hospital committee was Mr L. Davies of Llandinam, whose great interest in health and peace were well known.

Under his leadership, the Association had co-ordinated the efforts of private individuals, central and local government authorities to deal with TB in Wales and Sully Hospital is a lasting monument to its enterprise, philanthropy and purpose.

The hospital was opened on Friday, November 6th 1936. Many of the first patients were thin the advanced stages, so the number of deaths was unfortunately large. In other cases, because the treatment was limited, many patients remained in hospital for two or three years.

It was built on 94 acres of land, of which 69 acres were foreshore, between Sully and Barry, facing the Bristol Chanel.

Sully was designed with the idea of forming traps for "sun heated air", and to provide shelter, not only from the southwest gales but also from the extreme heat of the afternoon sun.

It had 300 beds with each unit containing 50 beds. These were divided into 2 x8 bedded wards, 6 x4 bedded wards and ten single rooms.

Furniture and decoration

There were many interesting fitments ahead of their time such as built-in wardrobes and bed headlights. The leading edges of doors were rubber edged to exclude draughts and most corners were curved to eliminate dust traps. There were dishwashing machines to sterilise crockery and cutlery, with a refrigerator and a steam heated kettle in each ward kitchen.

On the other side of the corridor were the patients' service rooms and toilets. Fireplaces were provided in the day rooms in addition to the central heating provided throughout.

The architects designed a large proportion of the furniture so that it harmonised with the colour schemes and modern architecture. Where possible furniture and equipment were standardised so that good quality materials could be obtained at a reasonable cost.

From July 5th 1948, overall administration became the responsibility of the Welsh Hospital Board. Locally, this was the Cardiff Hospital Management Committee until amalgamation with Cardiff North in 1972 and South Glamorgan Health Authority in 1974.

Soldiers from Dunkirk

Non-TB cases were admitted after the Second World War but in 1941 the Emergency Medical Service requested further beds. It is believed that a number of Dunkirk wounded were in Sully from 1940/41.

One day during the war

An unexploded bomb dropped adjacent to the existing mortuary and staff on their way to breakfast next morning inspected it. Shortly after they entered the hospital, it exploded.

New drugs

By the late 1940s the use of new anti TB drugs and advancing techniques in surgery and anaesthetic were having a marked effect on the treatment and prognosis of patients. Amongst other advances being devised was the "Sully Method" for the treatment of primary TB in children. To keep up with the increasing demand it was found necessary to appoint a pharmacist and physiotherapist and to provide an additional operating theatre and postoperative ward.

Surgery

The hazards in lung surgery for TB had been largely reduced and the need for such operations also lessened but unfortunately there was now a need for such surgical interventions for lung cancer and heart surgery.

Technical staff

Between 1951 and 1962 the medical laboratory technicians had increased to a technical staff of seven, plus a pathologist. The first occupational therapist was just part time after the war and an art therapist started in 1952. A dietician also helped in the treatment of patients.

Religion

In 1953 the chapel, served by three chaplains, was opened.

Volunteers

A survey of the hospital would not be complete without mention of the voluntary services. They organised a range of amenities for both patient and staff including a Samaritan telephone trolley service, a bungalow for the relatives of seriously ill patients and throughout the years the W.R.V.S and the Red Cross Society provided a valuable service.

International recognition- 1960s

Sully was to achieve its peak performance and attain international recognition around the mid 1960s. At this time the Hospital Social club came into being, and the staff spent many hilarious hours digging out the swimming pool.

Closure

Under reorganisation of the health services, many of Sully's pioneering projects were transferred to Cardiff, and the hospital eventually became an outpost offering facilities for geriatric and psychiatric patients before finally closing its doors in 2001.

(Source - Sully Hospital 50th Anniversary committee, Glamorgan archives)

Chapter 1
Searching for Sully

We circle Cardiff airport, and I slacken my seatbelt to get a better view of Sully hospital, an isolated tongue of land jutting out into the Bristol Channel.

Only it's no longer a hospital but an exclusive upmarket apartment block. The year is 2009.

Many years have passed since I was a patient here. Today I am returning, a ghost from the past, to write its history.

What will I find?

I pick up a hired car, and drive the few miles down the road to Sully.

It is also an opportunity to fill in another piece of missing Welsh social and medical history. This was chronicled in "The Children of Craig-y-nos" a book about a children's sanatorium deep in the Swansea valley where I spent four years as a child.

Nothing had prepared me for the difference in Sully then, or now. If Craig-y-nos Castle, represented all that was dark, cold, and austere, the traditional way of treating TB until the invention of the life-saving drugs, then Sully was the opposite: light, air, warm and progressive.

A smooth salesman emerges from the on-site show office.

Am I interested in buying?

No, I shake my head. He wears dark glasses. I find this uncomfortable, not being able to make eye contact.

I want to tell him my story, my search for the lost memories.

"I am an ex-patient," I say. Even behind the dark glasses I sense his face muscles tighten.

"Really?"

Clearly he does not want to see former TB patients turning up in his office. They give the wrong impression. I sense that.

I have come a long way. From Scotland. I am not going to be put off by his manner.

"I am going to write a book about Sully, about the time it was a hospital."

"What for?" he almost snaps his reply.

This time I go into journalist mode. I have not survived over 30 years working in Glasgow as a journalist, one of the toughest cities in the world, without developing an armour plate exterior.

"I would like to see around the building."

He juggles a bunch of keys in his pocket.

"Follow me".

Clearly he wishes I was not there, an unwelcome guest from the past. There is no commission to be gained, no kudos to be earned through showing an old patient, and a TB survivor at that, around the new development.

We go upstairs, and all the time I am quietly marveling at the luxurious interior.

"I will take you to the show flat." He does not speak after that though I try to make conversation.

Finally he flings open a door.

"This is it."

I gasp.

It's my old ward.

Walls that were once empty are now decorated with big pieces of contemporary art. Instead of our narrow beds there are comfy sofas.

I marvel at the transformation.

The salesman is not interested. He is anxious to get away, to find a proper client. So I take some photos and leave.

My tour of Sully over, I bid good-bye to the salesman, with his bunch of jangling keys and dark glasses, convinced more than ever that there is a story waiting to be told.

So began my search for Sully's missing history.

In February 2009 I contacted BBC Wales South East and they placed the following appeal for survivors on their web site:

"As a teenager, Ann was a patient there for six months in 1960 when it was a tuberculosis hospital.

Some of the first trials for drugs that were to go on to cure TB were carried out at Sully.

Ann has already co-written a book entitled The Children of Craig-y-Nos about the Swansea Valley castle's time as a children's TB sanatorium.

Ann tells us more about her time in Sully Hospital:

"Sully. The word conjures up many meanings - depending on your age. If you are young it represents a luxury upmarket apartment block overlooking the sea, somewhere you aspire to live in.

"But those of us with older memories, going back 50 years and more, remember it for what it was originally built for in 1936 - a state of the art model hospital for TB patients.

"I was one of those, a teenager in 1960, sent to Sully and I remember the fear and dread it cast in my mind. Having as a child spent four years incarcerated in Craig-y-nos Castle - the children's TB sanatorium at the top of the Swansea valley, former home of opera diva Adelina Patti - we had lived in fear of Sully.

"It was where they sent you to die. It was where you went to have 'the operation'.

"So the news that I was being sent to Sully - instead of teachers training college in Bristol for I was in the Sixth-form at St Michael's convent, Abergavenny - plunged me into a state of total despair.

"For in the weeks waiting for a place in Sully I slept with a bottle of aspirins beside my bed. I looked at them longingly each night. My world had been destroyed. Again. Should I or shouldn't I?

"I'm glad I didn't. Within hours of arriving in Sully my fears dissipated.

"The sheer dazzling brightness and warmth of the place lifted my spirits immediately; so bright was it that I found myself blinking unable to believe it. And the view from the second floor overlooking the sea was breathtakingly beautiful. Immediately I felt better.

"I had left behind a lonely, cold damp farmhouse outside Crickhowell. Now I was in a ward that was bustling with life. And it was warm.

"Gone were the old sanatorium ways of treating TB with their emphasis on isolation and coldness with visitors once a month. Instead they were replaced with drugs, warmth and weekly visitors.

"I was to remain there for six months. And it remained a pivotal moment in my life, one that changed the course of my life for the better."

Chapter 2
Patient number 07313

"You were admitted to Gwynedd ward of Sully Hospital on 1st April 1960, your patient number was 07313; you were discharged after 147 days on 26 August 1960.

"The sampling of patient's case notes during the period 1954-1967 took only file numbers ending 01 or 51, unfortunately this means as your patient number did not meet these criteria your notes were not sampled for retention."*

Letter from Glamorgan Archivist, Glamorgan Record Office.

*The sheer number of patients made it impossible to record them all.

The shock of Sully startles me.

In the morning I leave behind a damp farmhouse, and an hour later I am in a ward with huge glass windows facing the sea, which seems to start at the bottom of the lawn.

Is this the place we feared so much during all those years in Craig-y-nos? The place you were sent to die? Is it possible that all those stories were not true?

It doesn't make sense.

My spirits begin to lift.

The sheer brightness of Sully, a 1930s art deco style "state of the art" modern hospital made of glass and concrete within yards of the sea, is a huge surprise.

I keep blinking, like some animal that has been kept in the dark and suddenly exposed to daylight, unable to believe this new world I have stepped into. Unlike Craig-y-nos Castle, a mock Gothic piece of architecture inspired by dark foreboding European castles, Sully comes out of the Bauhaus movement dedicated to modernity and simplicity.

Built in 1936, it was designed specifically to combat the traditional prison-like regime of sanatoriums. Wards are named after Welsh counties and I am in Gwynedd.

I am dazzled by the brightness and warmth of the place; nothing had prepared me for this.

Is this the same place you were sent to if you had a few months to live? If you were one of the "no-hopers"?

In the early days that was certainly true. Few came out of Sully alive.

But the advent of drugs in the late 1940's changed all this, except for those who were resistant to them.

Indeed, by the time I was there the ground floor of Sully was already given over to heart patients where much pioneering work was done.

But the news of these medical advances never filtered down to us.

All the information we had was gleaned in a haphazard fashion from family and friends. There was no source of accurate medical information and you certainly dare not ask your doctor.

You accepted that they knew best.

So it was on the first of April 1960, I became the 7,313th patient.

My bed is next to the window with views over the Bristol Channel and the sea seems so close I feel I could reach out and touch it.

And the noise of the waves is like strange haunting music,

Then something strange happened. There was an immense lifting of the spirits as if into the sea passed all my fears.

It was as if the sea took and engulfed my pain, my diseased body, and my repressed emotions and transformed them into something elemental of its own.

The sick bodies came and were healed. Each let the sea take back into itself that part of the human spirit that hurt that twisted emotion, so the sea, all-possessive, hugged back all sickness.

The waves forever enveloped those who came to the white hospital on the seashore.

This strange feeling I had that first day never left me: indeed throughout my time in Sully it grew stronger if anything. It was as if the power of the sea and the architecture of the hospital were in themselves just as important in curing us as the daily drugs we were required to swallow.

But I digress. A nurse enters the ward.

She calls my name and orders me to follow her.

She takes me to the bathroom.

"Get in the bath!"

"But I had one this morning!"

"Never mind, you have got to have another one now," says the nurse, standing there with her hands on her hips waiting for me to undress.

"It's hospital rules. I'll sit here and watch".

She sits on a wooden stool besides the bath watching while I scrub myself.

It's also the rule to be searched for fleas and sores.

Back in my bed facing the sea, I am still unable to grasp my new situation.

Is this the place we, as children, feared all those years ago in Craig-y-nos, where the very mention of Sully evoked terror?

There are two other women in the room, both older, and a third bed, empty, next to me.

Introductions are made. Fast.

"You are still in school?"

"How old did you say you are? 18? you don't look it," says Lisa, thirty-four but looks much older.

Suddenly I realise I am something of a novelty: not only the youngest in Gwynedd block but an 18-year-old schoolgirl!

"Why are you still going to school?" they ask. I tell them about Craig-y-nos and about my hope of going to college. They are not interested. They want to know what's wrong with me.

Chapter 3
Lisa and Megan

Lisa, I discover, left Ireland as a young woman of twenty-one with £30 in her pocket in search of a new life in England, except she got no further than Cardiff, where she got a bed-sitter and a job on a market stall.

But all that standing around outdoors in all weathers and constant bouts of bronchitis aggravated her "bad chest", something she had suffered from all her life.

Once Lisa must have been very beautiful in the way Irish girls are, with her long red hair and luminous green eyes. To-day she is prematurely haggard with deep wrinkles and she is forever brushing her hair, frantic that this vestige of her former beauty will disappear too.

Twenty-six year old Megan, spends her time writing letters home telling them how much she hates the hospital. It's her first time away from her family and she has been in one week. Both women are single.

"Just listen to me Megan", says Lisa, "after a couple of months here you will get used to it. We all do. There's no point upsetting your parents …" Lisa never gets to finish the sentence before Megan lets out a loud shriek.

"Months! I can't stick this place for another week, let alone a couple of months. It will kill me."

She sniffs and dabs her tears away.

"The doctor promised me I would be here for a month at the most."

Lisa laughs.

"You don't believe him do you? They always tell you that! They told me that I would be here for a week and I have already been in for over a year. Never believe a word the doctors tell you".

I keep quiet. I decide it is not a good moment to tell Megan I was in Craig-y-nos Castle for four years when they had assured me it would only be for three days.

Megan's crying turns to sobs. I watch, silent and stoical. There are no tears on my part for Craig-y-nos had turned me into a survivor. Now that the initial shock of discovering I had TB again was over, I no longer feared the disease. Pain and institutional life held no fears; indeed there was almost a feeling of security, of coming home again. I was no longer a social outcast. I was among like-minded people. There would be camaraderie, a sense of belonging.

No, what I feared most was the outside world, of not fitting in, of living forever on the fringe of society. Unwanted. Had I not grown up with the endless stories from my mother of how the rest of the family had urged her to leave me in Craig-y-nos? What was the good of bringing a child with TB back to a farm selling milk? I never did learn the truth of these stories, but there was no mistaking the logic behind them. In a farming community, there is little room for fine feelings or sentimentality when it comes to sick young animals. You make a decision. Will this animal be useful stock? If not, get rid of it. Quick.

So, it is a small step to apply that same logic too to a sick child. Certainly on the day that I left Craig-y-nos Castle I was surprised to find another member of the family, an aunt whom I had not seen for over four years, also in the car.

She had come to strengthen the family resolve that I should be "kept in a bit longer". But the staff at Craig-y-nos, to their credit, insisted I go home.

So what frightened me most when I got the diagnosis of the disease again, I knew I could cope with that, was the knowledge that I would be homeless. Where would I live? How would I survive?

So I watched Megan's tears with certain coldness.

Until a few weeks ago, she had led a quiet life as a clerk for a shipping company in Cardiff.

Then the mass x-ray unit came to the office. Just routine, except it was not routine with Megan. They called her back.

They told her she had TB. At first she refused to believe them. How could it be? She argued with them, she told them that only dirty, or poor people got the disease and she was neither.

She lived with her parents in a comfortable house on the outskirts of Cardiff. Her parents were proud of her. She had a job in an office. She did not have to go and work in a factory like so many of her friends from school. Then a few weeks later she got a letter telling her to report to Sully.

What's more, she neither felt nor looked ill.

Yes, she's angry, and upset.

"Nobody in our family has got it," said Megan weeping. She believed, like many, that the disease ran in families.

She was still sobbing that afternoon when I returned from my bath.

Megan pulls another one of the large white hospital handkerchiefs we are given and with one hand she mops the flood of tears pouring down her face, and with the other she writes a letter home, pages and pages of tear-stained anguish.

Lisa long ago stopped suffering from homesickness. For her getting diagnosed with TB and sent to Sully was a release, an escape from a world of poverty. TB offered a way out. She is warm and cared for. As for the future? Who knows?

She could not share Megan's anger.

But it was different for Megan. That visit from the mass x-ray unit had ripped her secure world apart.

Her head is full of stories told by older relatives and friends:

"No one comes out of Sully alive.... those that do are cut up and are never the same again."

Yes, I know those scary stories about Sully, frightening stories embedded in the collective memory of Welsh culture.

Once, in the recent past they were true, but the discovery of streptomycin, the miracle drug, changed that.

Edith, an elderly orderly, comes into the ward, giving out cups and plates for tea. (I note that unlike Craig-y-nos we are not required to have different coloured bits of wool attached so that we only use the same ones each time).

She points to the empty bed:

"In the old days that would be filled before it was cold", a reminder that despite the new life-saving drugs, memories of "the white plague" still linger.

This only serves to set off another bout of weeping on Megan's part.

Chapter 4
Quick medical diagnosis

That first day I undergo my first medical examination, not by doctors, but other patients, and it is to prove surprisingly accurate, though I do not know it at the time.

A never-ending procession of dressing-gowned figures walk in to see what I am like, for the arrival of a new patient is an event.

They ask the same questions:

"Is it true you are still going to school?"

'What's your name?"

"Where do you live?"

"How old are you?"

This is the small talk, the social lubrication, before they get down to the serious business: "What's wrong with you?"

Yes, we might all have the same disease, but it is the variations that arouse the interest.

"Which lung have you got it on? You say that you have had it before? Really! You don't look ill".

Another added: "Did you say a shadow on the lung? Well, I don't think it can be much. You will only be here for a few months."

"Do you spit?"enquired a third. "No, I didn't think you would. Well, that means you will have to have a 'gastric'."

"Are you negative or positive?" demanded another woman, who considered herself something of a medical expert.

'Does it run in your family?"she added.

"No."

"I must say those relations of yours looked healthy enough. Was that your mother and her sister?"

I nod, wondering what they would have thought if they had known that they had been scrutinised by patients for signs of TB.

The outcome of this communal diagnosis is that I will be in for a couple of months, during which time a portion of my lung will be removed.

Sully's reputation rests on: "if in doubt, cut it out".

And that diagnosis proves surprisingly accurate.

Long after the visitors had gone, two women stand out. The first is Catrin, wafer thin, like a walking skeleton and I find that I cannot take my eyes off her. Her face is ashen, corpse-like, made all the more grotesque by her determined efforts to try to hide the disease through make-up.

Her long nails are painted a brilliant scarlet and she kept using them to express her feelings. They only appeared to claw at the life ebbing from her.

And Suzie.

Even though I have been in Sully less than twenty-four hours I can tell Suzie is special. She is fizzing with life though she has had suffered innumerable breakdowns and despite an unfavourable prognosis, she keeps bouncing back to live a bit longer.

She's a human dynamo.

"Let's say I have seen thirty-five come and go," says Suzie teetering in on stiletto heels into our ward wearing a new emerald green dress.

She's come to be admired.

Suzie takes pleasure in revelling in her appearance knowing it's the cause of some jealousy though the women never show it, at least not until she leaves the room.

"Her husband indeed!" said Lisa. "Did you hear the way she talked about him? As if he still comes to see her! We all know that he has never been inside the place ever since he overheard on the hospital bus that she's been carrying on with a man from the male wards."

It is followed by a thin, spidery woman pointing out that she doubted, in her opinion, whether Suzie had long for this world anyway.

Lisa sniffs. "You must be joking! Those who live like the devil always survive. I always say that we'd get better quicker if we prayed to the devil than to God."

"Flirts with anything in trousers," added another.

"That's her third husband, anyway."

"I don't know. There are those she has married and those that the breath of law has not touched," said one woman who made no pretence to keep the disapproval out of her voice.

"Did you know that she doesn't consider her affairs that last less than a month as an affair? She tells you with her nose in the air that they are 'mere trifles, nothing but a cocktail.'"

"Oooh …… aaah!" breathe the women on hearing sex referred to as a 'cocktail'.

"She must have had a lot of cocktails in her life," snapped Lisa.

"And Dr. Serrano, that young Spanish doctor caught them at it the other day behind the rhododendron," another volunteered.

"She goes around brazen as brass saying that Dr. Serrano told them they ought to restrain themselves until they get out. She even went so far as to say, mind I do not know if it's true, that Dr. Serrano offered to give them pills to subdue their natural instincts if they felt the temptation too much. But she claims that she told him that her natural instincts were the best part of living."

A woman in a pale mauve dressing gown allows herself a thin smile.

"Dr. Davies would not be pleased. You know how particular the medical profession are where sex is concerned. Mind, they do say that this disease makes you feel more sexy."

"Rubbish! Suzie has no more control over herself than a rabbit," says Lisa.

Nothing the nuns at St Michael's Convent taught has prepared me for this world.

My book of poems by Keats lies unopened on my bedside locker.

Within hours of my arrival in Sully one name keeps recurring: Sister Riley. Have I met her? What do I think of her?

I shake my head, though I can't help noticing that her name is mentioned with a mixture of fear and dislike.

Chapter 5
Corpse material

Is she the Sully equivalent of Dr Hubbard, the terrifying Austrian Jewish lesbian who ruled Craig-y-nos?

The first time I saw Dr Hubbard I was just nine years of age and she so frightened me that I ran and hid behind Sister Morgan's skirt.

She seemed to be neither man nor woman: her top half with short back and sides haircut was very masculine but she wore thick stockings and a skirt.

Her breath stank of cigarette smoke and she had several gold teeth. She had a strong guttural voice and a foreign accent.

I remember her leaning forward, grabbing me and placing me between her legs. It was an alarming experience.

Would Sister Riley be a Sully incarnation of Dr Hubbard?

"You will see her this evening then," said Lisa. "She comes around twice a day, once after breakfast and again before supper."

That night to my surprise instead of looking into the face of another Dr Hubbard, a youthful looking middle-aged woman with startling green eyes confronts me.

What is there to be afraid of? I am shocked, though, at the intensity of her gaze: the way her eyes seemed to burrow into me. She doesn't speak, merely gives a quick smile and moves on.

Only later do I to learn the truth – the real reason she is loathed, hated, feared. For Sister Riley enjoys the process of people dying, of helping them on their way.

And plenty died at Sully before the invention of streptomycin. Sister Riley, the story goes, refused at first to believe it worked.

Maybe that explains her cursory dismissal of me that first evening.

I am not corpse material.

Chapter 6
The assault

On the Sunday evening of my first week, Staff Williams puts her head around the ward door.

"Which one of you is Ann Rumsey?"

"I am."

"Gastric for you in the morning. Remember, no eating this evening".

And she's gone.

Lisa explains the procedure. I nod.

Memories of Craig-y-nos come flooding back. Yes, I know all about gastrics though I say nothing.

Maybe things have changed. After all so much else had.

Monday 6am. Staff Williams signals for me to follow her down the long corridor to the treatment room.

Lisa, in the next bed, wishes me luck. She promises to keep

me a cup of tea.

Staff Williams surprises me with a question:

"Can you do it yourself?"

"Do what?"

"Oh God! Don't tell me you're a new one?"

"Yes."

"Just my luck to get a new patient on a Monday morning. Well, I'm very busy so let me tell you straightaway that I'm not going to stand for any nonsense."

With that she proceeds to unravel what looks like yards of thin orange tubing.

I have already made up my mind that swallowing it would be impossible. I remembered the fight at Craig-y-nos, how the nurse kept struggling until my spirit was finally broken and I would sit there in the bed, tears streaming down my face, oh no I knew about gastric lavages.

I do not tell her about Craig-y-nos.

"I will show you this morning but I hope that for the rest of the week that you will be able to do it yourself," she says.

"The idea is that you swallow this until it reaches your stomach then I take this syringe and draw fluid off. Do you get it?"

I nod.

"How do you know when it has gone down far enough?" I am playing for time before the inevitable battle begins.

"I guess. I've been doing this job long enough that I can now tell within half an inch. Are you nervous?"

What a silly question! I nod.

"I warn you. I don't stand for any nonsense. If you do exactly as I tell you it will all be over in five minutes. If not it will drag on for half an hour."

She advances to where I sit perched on a high chair, the orange tubing dangling over her left arm.

"Open your mouth!"

There follows an extremely unpleasant twenty minutes during which the nurse becomes more and more angry.

She makes a decision.

She puts the tube back on to the kidney shaped tray. For a split second I think she has given up.

Until she turns to face me with a look of pure hatred in her face, such hatred that I have never seen in another human being before.

She walks slowly towards me.

Then it happens: a series of short, violent slaps across the face.

I fall off my stool.

"That will teach you! You silly little bitch! I warned you that I wouldn't take any nonsense. Take that and that!"

The assault over, her anger vented, she relaxes and stands watching me.

Tears start to roll down my face. Humiliation, anger and fear swept over me. I am helpless to defend myself but most of all I hate the degradation of being ill.

She attempts the process again, and again it is a failure.

Now she changes her strategy.

"Right! If you won't swallow it then you will have to have it through your nose."

By this time I am such a state of shock I sit there frozen, motionless. The procedure, using this new method, is surprisingly quick and though uncomfortable, it was painless.

I return to the ward, shaken.

Lisa is waiting.

"How did it go?"

"Dreadful." I am still wiping the tears away.

"I've kept you a cup of tea. Here it is. Drink it up and you'll feel better."

I am grateful for the lukewarm tea and the kindness.

Lisa offers advice:

"Do it yourself. It's less frightening. Anyway, the staff much prefer you to do your own. They don't like the job either."

During the next twenty-four hours I rehearse the procedure in my head. I have made up my mind. Even if it takes all morning I am determined to do it.

Next day in the treatment room, after a sleepless night, I tell Staff Williams of my decision.

She's not interested.

"Please yourself. There's the tray. Get on with it. I will be back in ten minutes."

And I succeed.

Chapter 7
My new social life

After this dreadful start my first week in Sully life begins to get better and I meet some of the people who are to be my close companions in the months ahead.

Like Dilys, the ward orderly.

She's plump, popular, single, and middle-aged, a woman who seems more like a loveable overgrown child, forever eating sweets and fruit. She believes in fate. She never bothers to wash the apples, so unlike the other orderlies, because she reckons that if you are going to catch the disease you will.

"I'm not afraid," she says.

Every morning Evans "the paper", a dark, short, cheerful Welshman delivers the morning papers and weekly magazines around the wards, carrying them in a large satchel on his back.

He believes part of his job is to cheer people up as well as sell them newspapers and magazines

"Hello, hello my darlings. What can I do for you today? Oh,

I see we have a new member to our holiday camp," he says, looking in my direction.

He gives a big smile, revealing several missing teeth.

"What would you like?"

He reels off a list of comics.

"*Jackie, Girl, Beano..*"

I am horrified. He sees the shock on my face.

"OK, maybe not. You are a bit old for them."

Just to drive that point home I ask for *The Spectator*, a recent discovery of mine.

Evans, "the paper", stops ferreting through his bag.

"I have never been asked for that before. Is it a romance?"

No, I assure him *The Spectator* is not a romantic journal.

"Well, I don't have it."

He delves again into his big bag of papers and thrusts an armful of tabloid newspapers in my direction.

"How about one of these for today?"

Only just in time, aware that Megan and Lisa are watching, and they have both just bought tabloid newspapers, do I stop myself from saying: "I am not buying any of that rubbish!"

Instead I smile and say: "No thank-you".

Phew!

For my convent education has turned me into a little prig, something that is going to get knocked out of me in the months ahead. Not that I realise it at the time, except I could sense how the nuns would disapprove of both Evans "the paper" and his bag of reading material, and the conversations of my new fellow patients, "So common!" I could hear Sister Philomena's voice even now.

No, the nuns would not approve. Were we not reminded never to eat in the street: "So unladylike my dear!" so I don't know what they would have made of sex in the bushes.

As for smoking, I knew their views on that.

Hardly a month went by before they would dismiss such practice sniffily:

"So vulgar!"

So I never did smoke, not on grounds of health but because of that strong indoctrination from the nuns.

Several weeks pass before I overcome my convent installed inhibitions and I join the daily smoking parties in the women's toilets, more out of curiosity than a need to conform.

After all, what did go on in there?

Despite the big notices displayed in wards and corridors, *Smoking strictly forbidden*, it went on every day. There were two main sessions, the first after breakfast and then again after supper. An unwritten understanding existed between staff and patients that the privacy of the toilets was respected during these times.

The first time I walk in on one of these smoking parties, the density of the smoke and the sheer numbers startle me.

"Move over!" urges one woman. "We've got a newcomer today."

So they make room for me. I squeeze in on the window-ledge, grateful that I am so thin.

How on earth do so many women manage to cram into such a small area?

Several offer me cigarettes. I refuse, not on health grounds because the dangers were unknown then, but because I consider it common to smoke, a view I keep to myself.

I stay. I am curious. The talk is women's talk of men, babies, home, boyfriends, going home, getting better and the future, that vague undefined area, uncharted waters.

This morning there is a new bit of gossip circulating: "Did you know that Miss Griffiths goes to bed with a banana?"

A stunned silence followed by screeches of laughter greets this piece of news. This is even more shocking because Miss Griffiths is a teacher and occupies one of the single wards kept for middle-class women and we think she ought to know better.

Chapter 8
TB patients over-sexed

Romances flourish even though men and women are segregated. A thin stream in the hospital grounds marks the boundary between the men and women's sections and I am told there is a large notice:

'Patients are strictly forbidden to cross the stream'.

But quite a few men and women jump the stream during their half hour of obligatory exercise in the grounds.

During my time in Sully I never left Gwynedd ward, or even got dressed, and fifty years were to elapse before I walked the grounds on a return visit.

There was a medical belief, (fact or fiction? nobody knows) that T.B. patients are more oversexed than normal men and women, and it would be considered highly irresponsible to encourage such meetings between the sexes, even outdoors. But women like Suzie ignore such hospital regulations. She arranges regular meetings in the hospital grounds with a man she waves to with her coloured handkerchief from her balcony every morning. He waves back.

In fact, one of the first things that Suzie did when she arrived was to invest in a pair of binoculars so that "I can see what I am getting."

Other women take a more romantic view. They wave their large white hospital handkerchiefs to the men in dressing-gowns in the hope that one will wave back. When a man does this, it's greeted with much excitement and laughter. The next step is the exchange of letters.

But Suzie has a grievance.

She tells us about it during our early morning smoking session.

She stands with one hand on the lavatory door and her other hand placed on her hip.

"My old man has not been to see me for six months. Do you think he's left me?"

Suzie does not wait for an answer but adds a quick 'Must go in' and darts inside the toilet clutching her small tight belly. There is a pause, broken only by the sound of Suzie peeing, then Dorothy, a woman in her early twenties, generous, good-natured and slow of speech, voices the thoughts of the gathered women.

"If my Bill hadn't been to see me for a month I would think there was something wrong. But six months, I reckon he's a gonna."

"What should I do?" asks Suzie, not that she would take any advice offered. A few make non-committal remarks. After all it is common knowledge that Suzie is having an affair.

"More than likely he's found out about you and George in the rhododendrons," says Megan.

"It's laurels not rhododendrons," says Suzie.

Megan shrugs.

"Whatever."

"Anyway, Bill ought to know me better. He knows my little weaknesses".

"Is that what you call it? said Lisa.

Suzie ignores her.

"I'll write and tell him not to bother to come to see me again. I'll tell him to take all my things to my mother's house."

"But do you still love him?"

I blurt out the question.

Suddenly, the women burst out laughing. I am mortified. What's so funny?

"Love him?" Suzie makes a funny noise in the back of her throat. "When you reach my age and have been through what I have been through you don't have much faith in love. If you can find a little comfort, a little spark of human warmth to share a few hours with, then that is all I ask. It's not much but it's worth a lot to me."

Another one, even more naïve than me, says: "When I get married it will be for love and a lifetime together. I will know it the minute I set eyes on him. Something will click.

And I will know he is Mr. Right."

This statement is greeted with even more ridicule and much laughter.

Undeterred, Mary continues: "I won't care what his job is or his background. As long as we love each other then that's all that matters."

Suzie tosses her auburn hair: "Don't let me disillusion you. Love and marriage isn't like that. You start with love then you discover it doesn't last and you get tired of each other."

In the weeks that follow I become a regular member of the smoking sessions though not actually smoking. (I try it one morning, urged on by the others, and nearly choke.)

These twice-daily meetings become like tutorials in "Real Life" and I listen, fascinated, as this new world unravels before me, a world never hinted at either at home on the farm or by the nuns in the convent.

All the women come either from the valleys, or Cardiff.

I am the only one from a rural background. And it shows. I am incredibly naïve and socially inept.

They speak of a world I could only begin to imagine. And they seem to have an unquenchable love of life.

There is never any question whether you have sinned that day, and have remembered to ask for God's forgiveness.

Chapter 9
Smoking, food and flowers

Staff Evans, against hospital rules, allows us to wash our hair after supper and supplies us with a hair dryer.

In return we stand guard in the corridor while she sits in the kitchen smoking with her cup of tea. A few weeks ago matron installed a large pane of glass in the kitchen door in order to deter such activities on the part of staff.

But it takes more than a piece of glass to stop Staff Evans. In fact, it makes it easier for the person acting as 'watchdog'. You simply give the pre-arranged signal, a dropped magazine or newspaper, and Staff Evans stubs out her cigarette, brushes down her apron and strolls out of the kitchen.

Sister Riley is ferocious in her attempt to stamp out smoking amongst the staff and it is rumoured that even gentle pipe-smoking Dr Davies puts his pipe out before coming on to Gwynedd ward.

One day we have fish cakes for dinner. I leave half. Having

been brought up on a farm I have never tasted fish and I have some very bad memories of fish from Craig-y-nos.

What will the nurse say? Will I get a row? I wait in expectation of a ticking-off at least. Nothing happens.

Young nurse Sally Jones takes the plate away without a word, not even a frown of disapproval.

I remark on this to the others in the ward. They don't know what I am talking about.

"They can't force you to eat it if you don't want to," says Megan who often leaves half her food.

She does not know, and I do not tell her, of the dark stories from Craig-y-nos where children would be force-fed food until they were sick, or of food returning for the next meal if left untouched as happened to me on one occasion many years ago.

Neither do the staff shout, punish or harass us, with the exception of Staff Williams and the incident with the gastric lavage, an isolated secret event.

As for the doctors we rarely see them and they seem kind, gentle and civilised, even putting a screen around our beds if they come to visit.

No, the biggest shock is not the regime of Sully itself, which is more pleasant than I had dared to expect, but the adult world of women into which I have been thrown.

Being ill is a minor matter in the day-to-day routine; after all, one feels well. Much more important though is the emotional atmosphere, the state of one's relationships with other people. An unpleasant remark from Sister Riley, and they are many, would upset someone for hours whereas a peaceful, calm atmosphere spreads ripples of contentment.

Take today.

Megan spent some time arranging a vase of red and white carnations brought to her by her mother. She placed them on the window so that we could all share them.

Staff Evans saw them through the glass window of the ward door.

She rushed in.

She snatched them out of the vase.

"Blood and bandages! Don't you know it's unlucky? Never, never let me see you putting red and white flowers together again!"

With that she separated the flowers in two vases.

They no longer look so pretty.

I wander into Ward 3, more for something to do than anything else. Only two in bed there, Mary, the hopeless case: "I knew I had the bug again but I was too scared to go to the doctor and now it is too late," she tells me with quiet resignation in her voice.

I turn away.

And Ruth, an old woman with one plait and one tooth. She is tucked away in a corner. Nobody is interested in her. She smiles at me. I nod. I don't know what to say.

There's an empty bed next to her. It belonged to Paula, only nineteen years of age. She was taken away yesterday morning, unconscious, to another hospital.

Today she's dead.

Vera from Ward 1 teaches me how to do the special knitting stitch for the dolls, which we are all making, a craze sweeping through all the wards.

What we do with the dolls once we have made them is less certain.

Chapter 10
To cut or not to cut?

Weekend visiting is over yet there is an unexpected air of excitement.

"Did you hear about Winnie?" says Cynthia popping in from next door. "She's going to discharge herself! Look, there she is in the grounds with her husband."

We climb out of our beds and rush to the window.

"He's been trying all afternoon to persuade her to have the operation. She won't! She says she would rather die first. Sister Riley told them they've got to make their minds up tonight."

Winnie is unpopular, for she has a malicious tongue.

Now she is walking round and round the grounds, arm in arm with her husband, their heads bent.

We watch.

Crowds gather in our ward to watch their slow progress for we have the best view of the grounds. Will she or won't she?

There's a ghoulish anticipation in the air.

"I hope he makes her have the op," says Dorothy.

Everyone wants to see her suffer.

It is getting dark, almost 8 o clock before they come in. They go straight to Sister's office.

Half an hour later Winnie comes into our ward, her face beaming, revealing her yellowed teeth with three gaps.

"I'm going home …… tonight," she shouts.

We are shocked and disappointed. We want her to have the operation, less because it would save her life but more to see her suffer though none of us will voice such thoughts. Yet they are there, unspoken.

"Are you sure you're doing the right thing?" asks Lisa.

"I don't care," said Winnie. "I'm not having an operation. Sister Riley has given me my medicine, and I have promised to take it every day. Well, bye everyone …'

With that she's out of the door.

Gone.

Winnie is visiting each ward to tell them the news, for like all good storytellers, she is aware that what she is about to tell them is dynamite. People who sign themselves out are writing their own death warrant.

And she doesn't care.

Within half an hour Winnie leaves under a stormy sky, arm-in-arm with her husband.

And two gallons of PAS. *(para-aminosalicylate sodium, a drug used to treat TB usually with streptomycin. Foul tasting.)*

Chapter 11
Ghosts in the machine

PAS ("tastes like cat piss") makes me retch. I have only got to see a medicine glass and I feel sick.

Edith, the orderly, reprimands me.

"If you had seen what I have you'd drink gallons of PAS. Fifteen years ago the women were dying like flies in here and not a drug would touch them. Drink and be grateful."

Terrified, I do for the rest of the day but by the following day my fear has worn off again and I start heaving when the medicine trolley appears.

It's Edith who tells us more of Sister Riley's sadistic streak.

Some attribute her unpleasantness to being jilted in her youth. Even the head surgeon is said to be afraid of her and puts his pipe out before going on to her wards. Now a woman in her late forties, Sister Riley exercises rigid control over her block of wards.

"She doesn't like people, she doesn't like animals, what on

earth does she like?" demands Megan.

"Illness, if you can call that an interest," says Edith, giving out the cutlery for supper. "I've worked here with Sister Riley for the past fifteen years and I know that you won't find any affection in that heart of hers."

"They say you only interest Sister Riley if you are going to die," added Lisa.

"Did you hear about the occasion when she took a group of visitors into Ward Six? They were a pretty groggy lot in there, it's true, but when one of the visitors turned around and said, "Your patients look really well, Sister."

Sister Riley smiled at the women in bed and said in a loud voice: "Yes, they're like rosy apples with rotten cores."

Edith nods. "I know. That's the sort of thing Sister Riley would say. It's not that long ago the single wards were kept for the dying, and I can tell you that they were never empty. In those days few recovered here. If you only had a slight touch of the disease you didn't come to Sully in the first place. Well, everybody's turn came sooner or later to be wheeled from the main ward down to the singles, and then we knew the end was only a matter of weeks away.

"Women dreaded being moved. They knew they had not long to live. Some of them would scream and shout, asking to be left to die in the main ward. Those were dark and horrible days and it still gives me the shivers just to think about it. But Sister Riley loved it. She loved every minute.

'Edith' she would say in her high-pitched voice: 'I want your help to move this person into Singles. I think it's time for this one to go.'

"Well, I used to feel like an executioner. What could I do? I couldn't refuse.

"She would stare with a horribly fixed look in her eyes and a set smile on her face at the woman in the bed. Often the woman would beg just to be left for a few days more. I still have nightmares about it. I hear those women still begging Sister Riley for mercy, and she never once gave in. She used to say 'They will be dead in a month, or less, what does it matter?'

"You ought to have seen her face when the new drugs came out. She didn't believe it. In fact she refused to believe it. Of course, there had been drugs before, gold injections and such like but they never worked. Sister Riley thought streptomycin was another such drug. But she was wrong!"

Edith finishes handing out the knives and forks in silence. Nobody speaks for a long while.

Chapter 12
Settling in

All wards face the sea.

So we enjoy a grandstand view of it every day. If this were a hotel we would pay a lot of money for a view like this. No matter, after a few days most of us become oblivious to the view and most women are more interested in those male dressing-gowned figures on the balcony opposite for the hospital is designed in a series of "W" shapes so each bed will get a sea view.

Our floor, Gwynedd, is divided into four bedded and eight bedded wards with a row of single-bed rooms/wards kept for (a) posh women i.e. middle-class, (b) those who have yet to be diagnosed with TB and (c) those recuperating from major surgery.

Most of my time is spent in bed and I do not get to use the recreation room at the end of the corridor except once to watch the marriage of Princess Margaret to Tony Armstrong Jones.

All the kitchens, treatment rooms, bathrooms and lavatories are opposite and parallel thus ensuring patients get the best view of the sea.

There are no second-class patients when it comes to sea views. We are all treated to the same, irrespective of our social background.

The side of the ward opposite the window is fitted with built-in wardrobes except they are almost empty because we don't have any clothes. These are taken away when we arrive, and we only get them back either when we leave or we graduate to walks.

I got mine back the day I left.

Throughout my time in Sully I lived in my dressing gown, a common practice amongst those of us waiting for surgery. Once we had our operation there was a six-week recuperation then the order was given to send for our clothes and we would dress and leave.

Yet some women were dressed and would even go out for walks daily. It all depended what treatment regime they were on. It remained one of the mysteries of the Sully regime how this was decided.

Nobody knew. Nobody questioned it.

Most of our information on what was being done to us came from other patients. Certainly Sister Riley did not believe in sharing her knowledge with us.

So we guessed. Usually we were right. This was based on our shared collective knowledge..

Our day would begin with a tea party at 7.30 am in our ward.

(I can only speak for our ward for I have no idea what went on elsewhere.) Now Sister Riley never for a moment suspected we had these early morning tea sessions, and it was only made possible with the change-over of staff and a little bit of bribery on our part for hot water. Staff were always susceptible to a few cigarettes.

After breakfast the treatment trolley is wheeled in with drugs and injections. Some nurses are much better at giving injections than others, usually the younger ones would be more considerate, while the older staff members adopted a more gung-ho attitude.

Our days pass in a mixture of talking, reading and knitting. I make some attempts to keep up with the set syllabus for my A levels and I have the books on my locker top, something that annoys the orderlies whose duty it is to keep the place neat and tidy.

They would like to see my books put inside the locker. I resist.

Also, I like seeing my books. They remind me that I have a dream that one day I will go to college.

We amuse ourselves by talking, reading newspapers, sometimes books and knitting. Evenings pass watching television – not that we have it every night. There are only a certain number of television sets, bought from money raised by Friends of Sully.

They rotate around the wards on a supposedly fair allocation system, though we suspect we are cheated but don't know what to do about it.

Visitors come for two hours every Saturday and Sunday afternoon. Two to a bed are allowed (In Craig-y-nos visitors were allowed once a month for two hours on the first weekend of the month).

Some cousins visit me. They looked around the other beds and said in a loud whisper to my mother:"But they don't look ill!"

They never came again.

The outside world ceases to exist for us as we become more deeply ensconced in our white cocoon by the sea. Only the daily papers, the tabloid ones, give a hint of the world outside, not that we are interested.

Life inside Sully is far more riveting.

Sully was way ahead of its time, not that we realised it then, a world away from traditional sanatoriums with their austere environments.

Here everything is warm and sparkling white, even the sea with the sun shining on it glistens like diamonds.

We even have proper heating in the wards, unheard of in TB hospitals where the belief still persisted that a freezing environment destroys TB. Among the more bizarre "cures", so I am told, is running barefoot in the snow, bathing in icy waters, gold injections and exposure to snow. Certainly in Craig-y-nos we got plenty of snow on our beds, which were covered in green tarpaulin, and if we should snuggle down to get warm, the night nurse would haul us up again in the belief that the freezing cold night air would do our chests good.

Chapter 13
Nessie, the "party woman"

Nessie, the orderly, flings open the door of Ward 2 and there is a tremendous draught for the windows are wide open. We clutch our daily papers and magazines for fear they will be blown away.

She drags her floor polisher with her, swinging it into the centre with a flourish that would do justice to a ringmaster in a circus. The floor is so shiny that you can already see your face in it. Still it must be polished. That's the rules and it's Nessie's job.

"Hullo, my old buggers, how are you?"

Megan stops doing her crossword puzzle and Lisa puts down her paper. Nessie, I sense, is no ordinary member of staff.

She's a woman in her late thirties, tall, gaunt, heavily made up with dyed auburn hair.

I close my book on Keats for I have taken to reading Keats because (a) he had TB and (b) I want to impress my ward-mates (big mistake!).

There are no teachers on Gwynedd ward for I am the only one still in education.

"Come on, tell us the news," says Lisa.

"We're bored." She clasps her hands together and makes herself more comfortable in the bed.

Nessie needs no encouragement. I have the feeling she is what "nice" people would call common.

She pushes the polisher around the floor and wriggles her bony hips sensing our interest. She keeps us waiting.

"Oh girls, I'm in such a whirl…I don't know whether I'm coming or going."

"How does my hair look?"

"Marvellous," lies Lisa. "Never seen you look better."

Nessie pats her extraordinary mop of red curls.

"I am so glad…I have a date tonight. Are you sure it looks all right? The wind does get to it, twists it all over the place."

"No, it looks as if you've just come out of the hairdresser," says Lisa. That's a lie. It looks like a tumbled mass of uncombed ginger hair, a thought I keep to myself.

"I'm so glad. I had it done yesterday."

"Who is it?"

It's not her hair that arouses so much interest in the ward but her sex life.

"Alfie. Home from the sea for a fortnight. I must give him a good time, mustn't I? That's what he says to me last night and boy did I give him the works, he doesn't have to ask me twice.

Still men, what can you expect and I enjoy it as much as they anyway, well, most of the time, so what's to be done if they want it, then let them have it. It's all the same with me."

I finger my book of Keats' poems. Keats never mentioned this world opening up before my very eyes.

There seems to be no stopping Nessie.

"Keeps them in a good mood. Oh, but you should see Alfie. Bronzed all over, you would think he was an African. And I says to him 'did you have any African women while you were out there? and he just laughs and says 'what do you think?'"

There's a silence while we digest this information. It is an unknown world to both Megan and Lisa and they take a vicarious pleasure in hearing all the details.

"What happened to Mike and Joe?" asks Lisa.

"Oh, they're still around. Marvellous boys. So understanding. We all go out together of an evening then we go…" She stops and looks in my direction, decides I am too young and shrieks with laughter instead.

"Marvellous boys my Mike and Joe.

"I go out with them when my Alfie is away. At least I do when I don't have to baby-sit for that daughter of mine.

"Did you know I'm a grandmother six times over? She breeds like a rabbit!

"She's got her seventh on the way. I says to her 'can't you do something about it?' and she says her George won't leave her alone in the night and I says to her, 'Don't be so bloody stupid, get down there to that clinic and have something put in you, that will soon stop it.' 'But I'm afraid,' she says. So she won't do it.

"I tell her 'You do have sex just the same.' But she doesn't believe me. I wouldn't let no husband of mine make me have kids every year. She can no more afford six kids than I can a fur coat."

She pauses for breath.

"Where is your husband now?" asks Megan.

At the mention of her legal matrimonial partner, Nessie's face contorts.

"Don't mention that bastard to me!"

"Go on" says Lisa in a low gentle, wheedling tone.

"Last I heard of him was eighteen months ago: he was setting sail for South America. I hope they've kept him there. Remember that ship that sunk a couple of months ago down there? He might have been on it.

"I'm afraid to go down to the shipping office to find out if he's dead in case he isn't, and it would be just my luck to meet him alive as ever.

"No, I'm keeping quiet about him, if he is dead he is dead and if he isn't then I don't want to know. He might come back if I go looking. He doesn't want me, only for what he can get for free when he's drunk and I don't want him. I have got my three nice boys.

"Oh no, you have got to make the best of life that's what I say, once you are dead it is too late. Grab it with both hands and live it to the full."

Nessie swings around in my direction. "Don't let yourself be pushed around in this world. You do the pushing and get what you want."

'Well as long as you don't do anybody any harm. I'm a Christian. You're a Catholic aren't you?' says Megan.

Nessie nods.

"Sex and God!...I luv'em both."

Suddenly the ward door swings open.

It's Sister Riley, followed by a nurse.

"Yes, we have a spare bed in here. Will you tell Mrs. McGrath to move in?"

Our social lives are about to change.

Chapter 14
Arrival of Mrs McGrath

Mrs Maggie McGrath has been in a single ward for the past three weeks.

Once these used to be kept for the dying. Now, with the introduction of drugs, they are used for post-operative cases, middle-class women like Sarah the doctor's wife, Janet a physiotherapist and Miss Griffiths, a teacher and the occasional woman, like Mrs McGrath, whom the doctors can't decide what is wrong.

Well, for three weeks, she enjoyed the friendship of her new friends and shared in their social status within the hospital. It also gave her a glimpse into their world; one she knew nothing about for Mrs McGrath, had a fearsome reputation. She kept a pub, "The Rampant Lion" in Cardiff's Tiger Bay area.

Three weeks after entering Sully the doctors confirm their diagnosis. She has TB.

The news puts her in a filthy temper for she is about to be

downgraded both socially and physically.

We are nervous. We are already familiar with stories about Mrs McGrath.

Did she not announce the other morning during the smoking session in the lavatory that "only dirty people get TB"?

She did admit, though, that her smoking disgusts her new friends in Singles.

So, we view her arrival in our ward with some misgivings. How will she fit in?

"What the bloody hell are they doing, putting me in here?" she demands as soon as the ward door is closed.

We remain silent. Instead we examine Mrs McGrath. This is the first time we have had a chance to have a good look at her because in the lavatory everyone is pushed in together, all squeezed up, so that you never get a chance to see what the other women are really like.

Mrs McGrath does not fit your traditional image of a consumptive. At least forty years old, probably more, with jet black curly hair, black eyes, above average height, (well for a Welsh woman) and stocky. You suspect she is not above throwing a punch or two, and she has a loud guttural voice not at all like the lilting tones of Lisa and Megan.

She may only have been in Sully for three weeks, yet we sense we have a woman whose personality is going to dominate our lives in the months ahead.

How are we going to adjust to living with her? Adjust we must, because in communal living we all have to get along with each other.

Lisa is the first to speak.

"You must have got it or they would not have put you in with us. They would have sent you home instead."

Mrs McGrath ignores her. She begins unpacking her few belongings, bundling them without order into her bedside locker. We watch without speaking, the tension mounting, a state Mrs McGrath abhors for she has Tiger Bay coursing through her veins.

Silence does not exist in her vocabulary. That is for dead people and she is very much alive.

"The trouble is that they don't know what they are doing in this place. Nothing but a bunch of amateurs."

"If that's is the way you feel, you had better sign yourself out," says Megan.

Mrs McGrath ignores the challenge.

Instead she puts a big collection of bottles and capsules on top of her locker.

"What are they for?" says Lisa.

"I can't take strep."

There's a quick intake of breath all round the ward: so that's the problem! She's allergic to streptomycin.

Finally she admits, yes, she does the disease, albeit in a mild form.

"I haven't got the bugs proper, though at this rate I'm sure to catch it from you lot."

"Watch what you are saying! This is a negative ward," warns

Megan.

(If TB is in the early stages it is not infectious and it is deemed negative. Once it is more advanced it becomes infectious and you are labelled positive.)

"What's that?"

Megan explains the nature of the disease in some detail to Mrs. McGrath who is neither a willing nor an apt pupil. Until now, she was convinced only dirty people caught TB. and she is not about to give up this belief without a fight.

Next morning Sister Riley tells her that her drug regime will be increased.

"Who says they haven't got anything wrong with them now," says Megan, getting out of bed as soon as the drugs trolley has left the ward, to take a closer look at Mrs. McGrath's assortment of pills, which have doubled. The top of her locker looks like a chemist's shop.

"Do you know, you have got more than the rest of us put together," says Megan.

Mrs McGrath has no wish to be reminded of this, and ignores Megan as if she were some passing wasp.

After the anger and shame of discovering she has TB, Mrs McGrath is upset too over losing her new friends in "Singles", middle class women who are kept separate from the rest of us - even though they have TB.

With her demotion to our ward, they soon make it clear Mrs McGrath is no longer welcome in their rooms.

So Mrs McGrath consoles herself by revealing some of their

habits.

"Do you know Janet Jones sleeps naked?"

Mrs McGrath offers this titbit of social gossip as her first contribution to our ward, and we accept it as a peace offering.

"How do you know?" says Megan.

"I went in there one morning to wake her up and I pulled all the blankets off the bed."

"There she was, naked as a pin!" Mrs McGrath is still shocked at the discovery.

"I says to her 'What if something happened in the night and you had to jump out of bed?' Imagine how embarrassing it would be to be found without any clothes on, but she never took any notice of me.

"She says she prefers to sleep naked because she likes the feel of having no clothes on."

Well, this insight into Janet's sleeping habits shocks us too. Mrs McGrath is unable to tell us whether the doctor's wife and teacher also sleep naked so we don't know whether this is a middle-class practice or just something that physiotherapists do.

We digest this information in silence.

Chapter 15
Murder in Tiger Bay

Mrs McGrath and I are to spend the next few months in adjoining beds, a prospect I am not looking forward to for we have nothing in common: she keeps a pub in Butetown Tiger Bay, a notorious dockland area of Cardiff which even I, straight out of a convent, had heard of.

It comes as no surprise to find Mrs McGrath loves the more scurrilous newspapers, which I consider common, though I would not say so for fear of being thought priggish.

Just how big that gap between us is highlighted when Mrs McGrath reads out the details of the latest murder in Tiger Bay.

"Girl murdered! Head chopped up! Stabbed through the heart!'

She reads us out the full story twice, dwelling on all the gruesome details.

We listen, shocked.

Something puzzles me.

"Why did he cut her head off? She would have been dead already, if he stabbed her through the heart?'

Mrs McGrath lowers her copy of the "Daily Mirror", and fixes her dark eyes on me.

"Is that all you've got to say? A girl the same age as yourself is brutally killed and all you want to know is why did he cut her head off?"

"Yes," I insist, for biology had been my favourite subject in school. "She would have been dead with her head on, if he'd already knifed her.'

"I don't know," shouts Mrs McGrath. "And I don't care! Where is your compassion?"

If I had shocked Mrs McGrath by feeling mild scientific curiosity regarding the murdered victim, instead of sympathy, then it was nothing to what followed a few days later.

We were discussing the new foreign nurse, Anna, from France who had been insulted when Megan asked her if she had nursed before she came to this country.

"Certainly not! My parents would turn in their graves if they thought that their precious daughter had to work for a living. I have made a mess of my life now … poof!" she waves her arms about in the way that continentals do.

She adds: "Now I have to wash people and make beds, whereas once I had servants doing everything for me."

We are not certain whether we like Anna or not but then we have never met anyone from outside Wales.

While we are discussing this, Staff Evans walks in to borrow a match from Mrs McGrath; they both share a love of smoking.

"We were just talking about that new foreign nurse," says Megan.

"You mean Anna? I'm sure I've seen her somewhere before. I think it was in a pub I go to with my boyfriend," says Staff Evans, taking the one match and cigarette offered by Mrs McGrath.

I blurt out: "You don't go into pubs do you? Why, you don't look the sort and I didn't think Anna looked the type either."

Too late! There's a stunned silence.

Megan, Lisa, Staff Evans and Mrs McGrath look at me as if I had just arrived from another planet. Not only are these women fond of pubs but, oh my God! Mrs McGrath keeps one in Tiger Bay!

I am appalled at my indiscretion. I wriggle down in the bed hoping to make myself invisible.

Mrs McGrath is the first to speak.

"I've kept a pub for fifteen years and let me tell you something, there's is nothing wrong with pub life. A good booze-up is good for your soul. God Almighty from the way you just said that, you make it sound as if going into a pub for a drink is the worst sin on this earth.'

They laugh.

But I find myself asking the question: "Am I really narrow-minded? Could the nuns in Abergavenny convent be wrong after all?"

Chapter 16
Television and fresh air

The days slip by and we become accustomed to Mrs McGrath. Indeed her presence, now our initial misgivings are over, has surprising benefits.

Take the allocation of television sets.

Until her arrival, our ward never got its fair share of the four sets, which rotate around the ten wards. Or if we did, we would get the old ones with uncertain signals, or even the dreaded black and white set.

All too often, we are cheated out of our evening entertainment, and when we complain to the woman whose job it is to organise the fair rotation of the sets, she waves her list at us, goes into a lengthy explanation just nobody understands a word, then disappears.

We have been successfully manipulated, but we do not know how. But all this changes with the arrival of Mrs McGrath.

She is passionate about Westerns.

She makes it her job to see that not only do we get our fair share of the television sets, but we get the use of the best ones too. Whether we like it or not, we find ourselves watching "Westerns" though none of us would dare to complain, because we are now so grateful to get the television which sits there, like a trophy, in our ward two evenings a week, much to the chagrin of women in other wards who peer through the glass window in the door from time to time, the nearest they can bring themselves to showing their displeasure.

But nobody will challenge Mrs McGrath.

If an endless diet of "Westerns" is the price we have to pay for a contented Mrs McGrath, we accept it, for harmony in the ward is essential if we are to live together.

Mrs McGrath must be kept happy.

But she is easily upset, and she has a violent temper. Take the night of the late Spring gale, with winds of 60mph and the sea outside had huge waves so that sometimes we thought it would tumble on to the lawns of Sully.

Our ill-fitting leaky windows rattled alarmingly, forcing open our ill-fitting ward door.

Now we all know that when the wind blows in off the sea, the ward door refuses to close. What with the draught from the windows that don't close properly and the door swinging open, there is a mini gale going through our ward, though nothing compared to what those of us who have experienced life inside a sanatorium have been accustomed to over the years.

Compared to Craig-y-nos, life inside Sully is pure mollycoddling even in a storm.

But not for Mrs McGrath, whose bed is next to the door.

"I'll shut that b....door if it is the last thing I do!", she says approaching it with an armful of newspapers. She proceeds to jam them in and it really looks for a while that she succeeds.

But as the evening approaches, so does the strength of the wind whipping in from the sea.

"I'm not standing for this! I'll freeze to death," shouts Mrs McGrath when the door swings open for the umpteenth time.

She grabs the emergency bell and presses it hard, really hard. Nothing happens.

"I expect they're busy," says Lisa.

"Nonsense! More likely Staff Evans is drinking tea and smoking cigarettes in the kitchen," says Mrs McGrath, for she knows Staff Evans' habit of retreating to the kitchen in duty hours for a smoke. Sometimes it has its benefits, for Staff Evans is open to bribes. If we are prepared to stand guard outside the kitchen, she lets us have little luxuries like hot water to make illicit cups of tea.

"Well," says Megan, "all this wind will blow your germs away."

"More likely I will be frozen in my bed," snaps Mrs McGrath, grabbing the bell again.

This time it had the desired effect for, unknown to the rest of us, Mrs McGrath had given three short, sharp bursts on the hospital bell, signifying a dire emergency.

It brings Staff Evans sauntering out of the kitchen.

"What's wrong in here?"

A cursory glance around shows her nothing untoward is happening.

"It's me," shouts Mrs McGrath, beside herself with rage as she peers over the top of the bedclothes, which she has pulled around herself in the hope of gaining a little extra warmth.

"What's wrong with you?" Staff Evans advances towards her bed, almost in a menacing manner.

"I'm cold!'

"You are what?" Staff Evans stops.

"I'm cold!"

Now Staff Evans' face assumes a peculiar expression, certainly I would not have cared to be in Mrs McGrath's place. Sensitivity was never an attribute high on Mrs McGrath's list of personal qualities. She misunderstood the look on Staff Evans' face and launched forth into a monologue of her lone battle to keep the door shut.

Staff Evans listened with growing incredulity. I thought she was going to explode. She puffed herself out, something that she always did when angry, and it made her look even larger than her fourteen stones. (We know that because we asked her one day during our weekly weigh in. The hospital likes to make certain you are gaining a bit of weight. Each new pound is greeted with whoops of glee.)

"Do you mean to say that you dragged me in here just to tell me that you are cold? What do you expect me to do about it? Well, I can tell you something: you're not the first person to complain about the cold and you won't be the last. You had better get down in that bed of yours and stay there. If you stopped thinking about the weather for a start you wouldn't feel half so cold.'

With that Staff Evans marches out.

Mrs McGrath is speechless. We try to hide our smiles. By the time she recovers her powers of verbal abuse, Staff Evans is ensconced in the warmth of the ward kitchen, cigarette in one hand and a cup of tea in the other.

Chapter 17
Mistaken identity

The lights have long been turned out at ten o'clock and we are still chatting when the ward door swung open and in walks the night nurse, followed by three surgeons.

"Is Mrs. Lewis in here?" she says, swinging a powerful torch in the direction of each bed. We blink, like rabbits caught in a bright beam of light.

The sight of the doctors paralyses our memories. Lisa is convinced they have come for her, like thieves in the night. Megan and I can only stare with fascinated horror at the three white-coated men standing in silence in the darkened ward.

Meanwhile, the night nurse is convinced that Mrs McGrath is the elusive Mrs. Lewis.

"Aren't you Mrs. Lewis?" she says, moving closer and shining the torch right in Mrs McGrath's face.

The three surgeons close in around her bed. Now, Mrs McGrath is terrified of a needle and the thought of undergoing surgery by mistake makes her angry. Very angry.

She grabs a letter on her locker.

"See? it says Mrs McGrath. I am Mrs McGrath, not Mrs Lewis…."

"Oh so sorry," murmurs one surgeon, the youngest of the three, the other two merely shrug and walk towards the door, but not before Mrs McGrath makes known her views of the medical profession.

"They can't even get the bloody name right!"

The night nurse attempts to control Mrs McGrath's vitriolic outburst with reminders about 'good manners'.

Mrs McGrath ignores it.

The surgeons move on.

Eventually they find Mrs. Lewis. She's asleep in the ward next door. They prod her awake and tell her they are going to remove her lung in the morning.

Sometime after this incident, Megan, who loved practical jokes, came up with one that went down in Sully folklore.

Nurse Anne-Marie Jones, a new big, muscular woman, is a recent addition to the night staff and she has trouble remembering people's names.

Well, one evening, she came into our ward brandishing an injection.

She had the purposeful air of one who would seem more at home on a parade ground than a hospital. "Right then, which one of you is to have this?"

This is the injection given to a patient the night before an operation, to help calm the nerves and ensure a good night's sleep.

Silence.

The nurse repeats the question and adds with a veiled threat: "Which one of you is Mrs. Thomas? Come on now, I haven't got all night. Own up!"

Megan seizes the opportunity, remembering the incident with the surgeons a few nights ago.

"That's her!" says Megan, pointing to Mrs McGrath's bed. "She's the one that's having the op. tomorrow and she won't admit it. She is scared of the needle. You know the sort nurse?"

"I do, indeed," says Nurse Jones.

"One of those is she?"

She moves towards Mrs McGrath's bed.

"Afraid of a bit of pain are we?"

Mrs McGrath gives a startled squeal.

Suddenly Lisa and I realise Megan's plan.

"She always gives the day nurses trouble', says Lisa.

"I am not Mrs. Thomas," says Mrs McGrath. Unfortunately she does not have any letters confirming her identity on her locker top.

"There, what did I tell you? She's denying her name already and it's all because she is afraid of a needle," says Megan.

The muscular nurse advances closer towards Mrs. Mrs

McGrath's bed adjusting her syringe in the process.

'You've got worse than this to go through tomorrow let me tell you that, so you'd better make up your mind to co-operate now. Look sharp about it too, I've got six others to do."

"Do as you are told, Mrs. Thomas," says Megan, assuming an authoritative manner.

Mrs McGrath for once is lost for words.

She grabs her bedclothes and holds on tight to them.

Finally she begins to assert her identity.

"Taint me …... honest …… it isn't me. My name is McGrath. I swear on the bible.'

"Rubbish! Don't take any notice of her nurse. Her name is Thomas," says Megan.

"I know your sort," says the nurse in a commanding tone of voice. "I know how to deal with women like you. I warn you now that I don't stand for any fuss."

With that warning, she rips back the bedclothes, revealing Mrs McGrath's vulnerable and exposed body.

'Down with your pyjamas!" says the nurse.

"Not bloody likely!' shouts Mrs McGrath trying to grab hold of the bedclothes. "'It's not me! Bugger off!" The language becomes more abusive but nothing that Nurse Jones had not heard before though some of it is new to me.

It does not deter the nurse.

Indeed, she seemed to enjoy a fight and she rolls up her sleeves in anticipation, ready to combat the unwilling patient with physical force.

"Are you going to take your trousers down or not?" She gives the ultimatum.

"No, I am not, so you can clear off."

That answer clinches the matter.

If the woman is not prepared to remove her pyjamas then she will have to receive the injection through them. Judging the position of the thigh muscles with a professional eye, the night nurse swoops with considerable force into the lower region of Mrs McGrath's anatomy.

Mrs McGrath screams and the noise brings in Maggie the night orderly.

"God Almighty! What on earth is going on in here? It sounds as if somebody is being killed."

The night nurse retrieves the syringe with a satisfied pull. It was a difficult job well done and she feels proud of herself.

"Mrs. Thomas wasn't co-operating over her injection, that's all."

"That's not Mrs. Thomas" shrieks Maggie. "That's Mrs. McGrath! You've gone and injected the wrong woman!"

Now it is the nurse's turn to be astonished.

"You're not Mrs. Thomas… but… I thought…' her voice trails off and she looks uncomprehendingly around the ward.

"Of course I'm not Mrs. Thomas!" screeches Mrs McGrath, beside herself with rage. 'That's what I have been telling you all along."

Now the night nurse turns and blames us, above all Megan for encouraging her.

"I never thought for a moment Mrs McGrath would allow it to happen," says Megan stuffing her bed sheet into her mouth to stop herself laughing.

But she had not reckoned on the night nurse's strength and determination.

Mrs McGrath holds her body rigid as if it is about to explode with the newly injected chemical.

"What will happen? I feel queer already."

"You'll feel even more queer in an hour's time," says Maggie. "You know, nurse, it's not right the way you carry on. If Sister gets to hear about it, she won't half be annoyed. I know you are keen and all that but you really should be more careful".

The nurse storms out, followed by Maggie. "Lead me to the damned woman instead of standing there lecturing me," says the unrepentant nurse.

Once Mrs McGrath realises the only thing that will happen to her will be that she sleeps well that night, her anger rises to majestic heights. Happily the drug soon begins to take effect and much against her will, Mrs McGrath falls asleep.

Chapter 18
Lisa leaves

Weeks pass, and the serenity of our lives is broken with the announcement that Lisa is to be operated on in two day's time.

She is asked to get a relative to sign giving permission.

"I don't have any relatives, at least not in this country," says Lisa. "They are all in Ireland."

She lives alone in a bed-sitter in Cardiff. From time to time a neighbour pops in to see her as she has no other visitors. So she has no-one to sign the paper. Sister Riley merely notes it on her pad.

Lisa gets Sally, a young girl in the next ward who dreams one day of being a hairdresser, to cut her hair. She wants to look good on the operating table. Sally makes such a skilful job of it that we all book sessions with her.

The pre-operation rituals begin the day before, with Lisa being shaved followed by a hot bath in disinfectant, and an injection the night before.

At nine o'clock prompt we hear the trolley coming down the corridor for Lisa and she leaves with a cheerful smile on her face.

Patients are never sedated before an operation. The result is that they arrive in the operating theatre fully alert and they are required to hop on to the operating table. Then, and only then, does the anaesthetist render them unconscious.

Once, the story goes, a patient was so alarmed at watching the pre-op. procedure in the theatre, that she jumped off the operating table before the anaesthetist got to her and bolted for the door. She was caught and placed on the operating table. Since then, they have taken the precaution of insisting that a nurse accompanies each patient until she is safely anaesthetised.

The nurses have changed the linen on Lisa's bed and removed all her belongings.

Our fears are confirmed – Lisa will not be returning to us. It's the usual practice after surgery to put a patient into a single ward for a few days, then transfer her back into the main ward, but never the ward that has been her temporary home for the past few months.

Mixing between wards is forbidden, especially between those who have had surgery and those waiting for it.

Thus friendships formed are neatly severed.

We are sad to see her go. So Lisa moves out of our lives.

We have been told to expect a new patient in a few days. We hope it's somebody young and lively.

Chapter 19
An "Old hand" returns

The bed is waiting, all white and neat.

What will the new patient be like? Who is this woman we will have to share our lives with over the next couple of months?

It was important for our peace of mind that we should find her agreeable, though such is the effect of communal life that, given time, even the most disagreeable companions slip into a comfortable rhythm of shared lives.

Twelve o' clock arrives and there's a brief knock on the door and two short middle-aged women walk in.

"Hullo." they say and seat themselves either side of the bed.

We are disappointed. We had hoped for someone younger.

Which one is it? No matter. They are indistinguishable from each other; they could be twins, or sisters.

"Beautiful weather we are having," says Megan, anxious to start a conversation, for silence is something the Welsh abhor.

"Reasonable for the time of year," says the woman in a dark, navy coat. Her companion, wearing an identical coat but in a somewhat lighter shade adds: "I've known better."

We do not argue.

"We had a nasty shower yesterday," said Mrs McGrath.

"Did you?"

They are not interested in us. Strange. Yet one of them is about to become our companion.

"It's our rest hour, that's why we are lying here all clean and tidy", I volunteer by way of explanation.

"We know."

How do they know? I'm peeved. Passing on information to newcomers is a minor delight of mine.

"Have you met Sister Riley?" asks Mrs McGrath.

They nod, and smile. This is most odd. Why should the mention of Sister Riley bring smiles to their faces? Neither shows any nervousness that would indicate which one is soon to slide between the pair of white hygienic sheets.

Our curiosity increases. Which of these two women is the new patient? Neither looks very ill, nor very well for that matter. It could be either, or both except there is only one bed.

Mrs McGrath's dark eyes dart from one to the other.

Unable to contain her curiosity for a second longer, she fixes her eyes on the ceiling, drums her fingers together and says with a sense of urgency in her voice:

"You'd better get into bed then. After all, you can't sit there all day." She adds the final sentence almost accusingly, letting her eyes fall on each woman in turn.

They jump, startled, finally becoming animated.

"It's not us. It's our sister."

With that the door opens and another short, middle aged woman walks in.

"Isn't this lovely! It's my old ward. I'm Bronwen. I used to be in that bed three years ago" and she points in Mrs McGrath's direction.

We give a collective groan. An "old hand", the worst kind of patient we could possibly wish for, is about to move in.

We know what is about to come: changes that have taken place, people she has known, most of whom will have died, and her own medical history which is sure to be long and complicated.

We will have to listen to "the bad old days".

We are right. Within half of hour she starts on her medical history. Our interest in her gives way to dislike as the day progresses.

Bronwen is obsessed with her own medical problems and shows not the slightest interest in ours.

It is dinnertime next day before I notice, with relief, that she has started to repeat medical history.

Our ward becomes the hub of the social scene for the next few days, as patients from other wards come in to meet Bronwen.

She has a shared history with several who greet her with

tremendous warmth. Clearly Bronwen is popular.

Each new patient is subjected to intense scrutiny: family, medical history, marriage, husband, and children. We want to know everything, and I mean everything, about each new woman, then our natural Welsh curiosity will be satisfied.

I realise that my own arrival must have been a source of some disappointment, for I was a mere schoolgirl.

With each new visitor from another ward Bronwen recites her medical history all over again, so much so that I feel sufficiently proficient in it to be able to give my own rendition which I attempt to do, in order to speed the whole process up.

Bronwen slaps me down.

"This is my story and I'm telling it."

There aren't many operations or drugs she has not had.

"None of them worked."

Bronwen is not the least bit interested in our medical histories. I did try to tell her about mine but only got as far as going into Craig-y-nos as a nine year old before she interrupts me with a story of a relative of hers who died within two months of leaving there.

"And she had been in for three years, didn't do her any good at all."

Bronwen does not get her first medical inspection until late on her second night. She has spent the day propped up in bed wearing her best nightdress and hand-knitted bed jacket, waiting for the young house doctor to appear.

She has her medical notes at her fingertips and we are all subjected to numerous 'dress rehearsals' – not, of course, that Bronwen was not word perfect at giving a skilled rendering of them already.

It's the bits she has to leave out that worries her. She knows the doctor will not want to listen and she finds it difficult to compress her complicated medical history into less than five minutes. We are not helpful.

Anyway, with the onset of evening, Bronwen decides she is will not be getting the regulation first examination, so she disposes of her best pyjamas and bed jacket complete with frilly pink bows, and slips instead into a comfy set of floral flannelette pyjamas and a warm cardigan.

But at nine o' clock, a night nurse darts into the ward and swishes a pair of screens around her bed. And in walks a very handsome young Spanish doctor.

Bronwen is flustered. She starts to stumble out her medical history but Dr Serrano, the young Spanish doctor, informs her he has 'read all her notes' and would she please keep quiet and breathe deeply so that he can listen to her chest.

Despite the screens and in the silence of the ward we can all hear Bronwen's rattly chest.

Time passes!

A week has gone by since Bronwen's arrival and already some kind of harmony is developing between us. We have found that she is quite an acceptable companion, providing we do not mention operations. There can't be many that she has not had.

Chapter 20
The silk dresses

Catrin from ward three has taken to visiting us since Bronwen's arrival. They have known each other for years.

But this annoys Mrs McGrath.

"You can tell a mile off she's riddled with it, you can see straight through her. Why does she have to keep coming in here?"

"I'm not saying a word to her," warns Bronwen, busy knitting away.

"She's dying," snaps Mrs McGrath. "I don't want her in here, spreading her germs."

"Catrin is a real lady."

Yes, I had noticed she speaks differently to the rest of us. She has a gentle, unassuming manner and her voice is neither of the valleys nor of Cardiff.

I saw Catrin on my first day and I was startled too at her appearance for she looked like a walking skeleton.

"You can tell a mile off she is dying", repeated Mrs McGrath. "Why does she have to keep on coming in here?"

"Because she's a friend of mine," says Bronwen. "If I want my friends to come in to see me, then I shall have them in."

We have learnt that Bronwen's placid manner conceals a very determined woman. Sensing a difference and potential conflict Megan interrupts: "Did you know Catrin has a boyfriend?'

"What?"

Mrs McGrath is astonished. "You mean she's got a boyfriend at her age? She must be at least fifty and just look at the sight of her!"

"Why shouldn't she have a boyfriend?" said Bronwen.

"But …"

We know what Mrs McGrath is thinking. Will she say it?

She does.

'I mean to say … what man would want her? There's nothing there but skin and bone".

"I wouldn't be so sure of that,' says Bronwen. "Catrin may not be much to look at, but she is a proper lady, very refined and educated too."

Mrs McGrath does not see this as an asset, quite the contrary, for she has little time for education ("bloody waste of time").

"That doesn't make up for the fact she's a walking skeleton."

Mrs McGrath is of the opinion that a man is attracted to a woman purely by physical appearance.

"He never misses coming to see her every Sunday," says Bronwen.

Mrs McGrath sniffs.

Her husband had stopped visiting her some time ago on account of his "bad leg", and he couldn't walk up the stairs.

"God, if she can still get a man, then I'm sure I can," she fumes, walking across to the window swinging her big hips in a most aggressive manner and twirling a cigarette between her chubby fingers.

"You're married," I point out. "Isn't that enough?"

"Shut your mouth! You don't know what you are talking about. If I could get another man I would, and quick too," she spits the words out. "What the devil does he find in her?"

"He must find something or he would not travel fifty miles every Sunday to see her. You know those silk dresses she wears?" says Bronwen.

Mrs McGrath nods.

Both the quality and quantity of Catrin's silk dresses have not escaped her attention and it has crossed her mind on several occasions how Catrin comes to be the owner of such fine garments.

"He bought them for her," says Bronwen.

"He bought?....." the sentence is left unfinished.

Mrs MacGrath is astonished.

Her mouth drops.

Not even in the prime of her life had any man given her expensive presents, let alone silk dresses, for she had been easily satisfied.

Chapter 21
Negative and positive

Our early morning tea parties, at 7.30am, every day, are getting tense. It is all to do with Mrs McGrath and her fear of catching the disease.

"Why do these women keep coming in here," she says. It is Dorothy and Maggie she objects to most, for they join us each day to share in our tea and biscuits.

"You know why they come in. To wave to Dorothy's brothers," says Bronwen.

"And to eat our biscuits," adds Megan.

"They ought not to be here," says Mrs McGrath.

"Why not?

"They are positive. This is a negative ward."

We do a collective sigh. Mrs McGrath still fears catching TB. She has now acquired some basic knowledge about the disease and she knows that ours is a negative ward. Yes, we have TB, but it has not reached the infectious stage, while Dorothy and Maggie come from a positive ward.

"I don't want them in here breathing our air. I don't want their bugs floating around. I'm going to tell them tomorrow they can clear out."

Next morning she is in the kitchen filling up the teapot when Dorothy and Maggie stroll in.

We lay out cups out for six people. On Mrs McGrath's return Dorothy's fingers are already deep inside Mrs McGrath's biscuit tin, for it is her turn to provide them,

"Nice biscuits you got today," says Dorothy, turning to smile at Bronwen thinking she is the provider.

Mrs McGrath watches her demolishing the biscuits. She can barely contain her anger.

But neither Dorothy nor Maggie notice the sudden change in atmosphere for they are too busy eating biscuits, drinking our tea and waving to the men on the opposite balcony.

There is a rigid protocol on the segregation of the sexes except at certain times of the week when they are allowed to mix e.g. bingo and church services in the hospital chapel.

"Look, there's my brother! Who is that with him today?"

"That's a new man!"

We rush to the window to inspect him, except Mrs McGrath.

All eyes are on the balcony opposite.

"That's Peter. He came in last week. He is forty one years of age, married with two children and a patch in his left lung," says Maggie who seems to make it her business to know as much as possible about every patient.

In the natural course of events Mrs McGrath would have been interested, but today she refuses to be sidetracked.

She can restrain herself not a minute longer.

"This is a negative ward."

Both Dorothy and Maggie, if they hear, ignore the remark.

Mrs McGrath repeats it, only louder, adding,

"You are positive. Both of you."

This time Dorothy takes notice.

"Of course I am. The bloody bugs are crawling in me."

She gives a cough to prove it, then takes another biscuit and helps herself to an extra spoonful of sugar in the tea, again supplied by Mrs McGrath.

She would have taken another biscuit if the tin had not been snatched away by Mrs McGrath and the lid slapped down.

"There won't be any left if you go on eating them at this rate," she said putting the tin in her locker.

There's an embarrassed silence broken by Mrs McGrath saying in a loud voice: "I don't think you should be allowed to come in here. This is a negative ward. We have ourselves to think about."

An uneasy stillness hangs in the room. Dorothy and Maggie finish their tea and leave.

They do not return the following day. Instead, the word spreads throughout the wards of Mrs McGrath's fear yet again of catching TB.

Our ward becomes ostracised. People stop coming in, and our social life is diminished.

Chapter 22
Mrs McGrath – slippers and sex

Women no longer come into our ward like they used to, for the story has got around that Mrs McGrath is afraid of catching TB. She keeps telling everyone she hasn't got it and she is sure to catch it from folk coming into our ward all the time. So suddenly life has gone quiet. Just the four of us. Except for Dorothy. She is oblivious to Mrs McGrath's stares, and rudeness.

"Have you got TB?"

"Yes, riddled with it," says Dorothy, giving a consumptive cough to prove her point.

"You shouldn't be in here. This is a negative ward."

For a woman who only a few weeks ago knew nothing about TB, Mrs McGrath has all of a sudden become an expert on the disease.

Dorothy ignores her. She sits herself down on Bronwen's bed.

They both share a love of knitting.

"Why are you wearing those heavy shoes?" demands Mrs McGrath, determined to needle her. Dorothy is wearing a pair of sturdy lace up brown shoes.

She laughs.

"Because I haven't got a pair of slippers. My old ones broke in half and there's not much chance of me getting another pair..."

She leaves the sentence unfinished.

"I'm getting used to them now. You get used to anything y'know."

"I've got a pair you can have. Open my locker and look on the bottom shelf," says Bronwen.

Dorothy is down on her hands and knees, and she soon has the contents of Bronwen's locker spread across the ward floor.

She finds the slippers.

"Try them on," says Bronwen.

Dorothy slips one on before Bronwen has time to finish issuing the invitation.

"They fit like a glove. Are you sure you don't want them?"

"No of course not. Leave them with me and I will stitch the hole in the toe. That's all that's wrong with them."

The door has no sooner closed on Dorothy than Mrs McGrath explodes.

"Why are you giving her those slippers? They are far too good for her! I need new slippers."

Bronwen is firm.

"Dorothy's getting them. And that's it," says Bronwen in a tone of voice that we have come to recognise. She can be determined when she wants to be and this is one of those occasions. "If you want new slippers, you can afford to buy them. Dorothy can't."

We all come from Welsh working class backgrounds, but Dorothy is very poor. We know because she wears hospital clothes.

All her family have the disease, and one of her children has just died from it. Her husband was admitted a few days ago and now he joins her other male relations on the balcony, the men who wave to us before breakfast most days.

Mrs McGrath laughs.

"You don't think I meant it, do you? For heaven's sake, I can afford to buy my own. I was only joking."

Nevertheless, her eyes continue to wander in the direction of Bronwen's red satin slippers and when she goes to the bathroom she rushes over and tries them on.

But they are too small.

Weekend visitors bearing presents lighten the mood

"It must have cost your village a fortune," says Megan, looking at the pile of gifts on my bed.

It's true! I do seem to have more than the others, especially Mrs McGrath who has neither presents nor visitors. She excuses her husband's non-appearance because he is busy working and can't leave the pub, though if truth were told he has a fear of hospitals, especially ones like Sully.

Anyway, one morning shortly after this, Mrs McGrath is to be seen watching the men on the balcony opposite. Our morning tea parties are now subdued affairs with just the four of us.

"I wish I was single again," she says, looking at the group of men in their dressing gowns on the far balconies.

"But why?" I ask.

Mrs McGrath breaks off her reverie and glares at me.

"It's obvious, isn't it?'

I shake my head. It certainly is not obvious to me, though I have by now begun to realise that there are many gaps in my life. A whole new world, which the nuns never so much as hinted at.

"I want a man. That's why I wish I was single again." She thumps the table with her fist to drive the point home.

Undisturbed by this violent reaction, indeed I feel almost triumphant, like one who has found the answer to another person's problems, I say:

"But you've got a man. You've got your husband. What more do you want?"

"Rubbish!" puffs Mrs McGrath, rolling her cigarette around her fingers.

"Anyone can see you haven't been around. Do you honestly think that after twenty years of marriage to the same man, you feel the same way toward him as the first time you got into bed together?'

"But your duty?" I murmur, for it is at times like this that my convent education surfaces.

"Duty!" shouts Mrs McGrath, as if I have mentioned some taboo word. "Do you think I can tell my body not to feel the way it does when I see a handsome man walk by because of my 'duty to God'? What about duty to my feelings and myself? I want to enjoy life. Why shouldn't I enjoy life?"

I remain silent.

Really, Mrs McGrath can be vulgar and I feel sure the nuns would not approve.

Chapter 23
"Do-it-yourself" gastrics

Bronwen, Megan and I are scheduled to have gastrics the same morning.

So at six o'clock, the night nurse appears with three bowls and a collection of syringes and tubing.

"You know what to do. Get on in with it."

And she disappears.

We have long passed the days of needing the privacy of the treatment room to carry out this medical procedure, which involves swallowing several feet of tubing and syringing the contents of your stomach off. In the old days this was fed to guinea pigs. If they lived, you were cured. If they died, you remained in the sanatorium. Sully used to breed guinea pigs just for this purpose. But by 1960, they had been replaced by laboratory tests.

The three of us chat while we sort out our bottles and syringes, and this wakes up Mrs McGrath.

She mutters from underneath her bedclothes:

"I hope you lot are not going to make any noise."

In order to carry out this particular medical procedure Bronwen and Megan have developed their own techniques, which does away with having to swallow two feet of tubing.

Their methods are unorthodox and noisy.

They force themselves to be sick by sticking fingers down their throats and then pour the contents of their stomach into bottles.

I begin the process of swallowing the tubing though I find it hard to concentrate with the noise of the other two trying to make themselves sick.

All this noise wakes up Mrs McGrath.

The scene that greets her, bleary-eyed as she sits up in bed and opens her eyes for another day in Sully, sends her into a rage.

It is true we are not a pretty sight.

"Get the hell out of here, the lot of you! You should be doing that in the lavatories."

"Oh alright" says Megan, who is not having much success poking her finger down her throat, and thinks moving to a new location might help.

Bronwen follows. So do I.

And Mrs McGrath forces herself back to sleep. So another day at Sully begins.

Chapter 24
Bingo and knitting

Thursday is bingo night, and it is very important in the life of Sully. This is the only occasion women get to see the men in dressing-gowns they wave to on the balconies every morning.

Ward 3 is buzzing with excitement all that day, for they are the ones with most men friends, never missing a morning waving to them from their windows.

Therefore, getting ready is not something left to the last hour, or even two hours. No, it takes up the whole day, what with hair washing, setting it in curlers, manicuring and painting of nails, and even bathing in perfumed water.

Some women confined all the time to bed have bath salts brought in by well-meaning visitors, a luxury they have no need of, which the women in Ward 3 are quick to spot after the weekly visiting. A little bartering takes place; some sweets or fruit are exchanged for these toiletries.

Once this is accomplished, there follows ironing and pressing of clothes, polishing of shoes and the final check of their outfits to ensure that nothing, but nothing has been forgotten.

At one minute to seven o clock, the Recreation door at the end of the corridor opens though the game does not start until 7.30pm (Ward 3 women always want the best seats) and I watch a procession of coiffured, smart, wafer-thin women teeter past our door on dangerously high stiletto heels, waving, smiling and full of hope.

Sometimes it is a disappointment. Other times women return to their wards delighted and full of hope. New romances flourish on bingo night and much letter writing follows.

I notice that all the women are very happy and contented for the next few days after bingo night, though the appeal of the game is lost on me. In fact, nobody from our ward goes.

Mrs McGrath did attend once, and came back disillusioned.

"Have you seen the men who play bingo for Chrissaake?"

She never went again.

Every so often a new craze sweeps through the wards. It could be anything from making gloves, doing crossword puzzles, to crocheting and needlework. Well, the latest is knitting and even Mrs McGrath succumbs.

It starts with Bronwen making an elaborate knitted doll's dress and now everyone is busy trying to make the prettiest and most complicated doll's dress.

Women come into our ward to admire Bronwen's knitting and the earlier unpleasantness involving Mrs McGrath and her fear of catching the disease are forgotten.

Now Mrs McGrath hates being left out. She wants to knit.

"I will teach you," says Bronwen, for she is a generous soul.

"I want to make a jumper."

"Have you ever knitted before?" asks Bronwen.

"I think you'd better start with a scarf."

"That's so ordinary…".

Bronwen, for once, is firm with Mrs McGrath.

"You start on a scarf and see how it goes."

Over the next few days Mrs McGrath keeps hopping out of bed, wanting help from Bronwen.

Now she is a very tolerant person, but all these frequent interruptions are causing her to lose her place in what has developed into a race for not only the one who makes the prettiest doll's dresses, but the most. All are destined to go as Christmas presents to children in Africa.

Well, within three days Mrs McGrath's scarf takes on a most peculiar shape, kind of lop-sided.

Bronwen, a perfectionist knitter, can stand it no longer.

"You've gone wrong. Somewhere. Let me count those stitches."

She does it quickly.

"You started with 120 stitches and now there are only 85," says Bronwen in an accusing tone of voice. The need for accuracy is lost on Mrs McGrath, who simply enjoyed the act of knitting.

And she watches with a clear sense of achievement as Bronwen holds the knitting up for us all to see. It is evident something has gone wrong.

The desire to create is one thing, having the necessary craft skills to execute it is another, something that Mrs McGrath has yet to learn.

She had hoped that her pleasure in knitting would overcome her lack of technical knowledge, or "the fiddly bits" and somehow it would all come out right in the end.

Bronwen, a woman not given to making quick or rash decisions, surprises us with the alacrity with which she whips the knitting off the needles and unravels Mrs McGrath's work.

"Don't do that! It's taken me three days to get that far!"

"But it's wrong," says Bronwen, unwinding the wool, demolishing Mrs McGrath's first creative handiwork and ego in one swift gesture.

"How can it come right of its own accord if you've gone wrong in the first place?" Bronwen asks.

But Mrs McGrath ignores her.

"You'll have to start again".

Of course, Mrs McGrath's difficulty with knitting does not go unnoticed. Women from neighbouring wards take a delight in Mrs McGrath's lack of knitting expertise. They saunter in, offering advice and some happen to have their own dolls in their dressing-gown pockets, which they produce for us to admire.

Some suggest she try something easier, though no one can think of anything that takes less skill than a plain scarf.

Chapter 25
The rotten apple

Yesterday Sister Riley went into Ward 3, the eight-bedder next door, on her evening rounds, stopping before each patient with her standard question:

"Anything to tell me?" only to receive the usual negative reply.

"No, nothing Sister."

Except Ruth, the hopeless case, the woman with one tooth and a long plait of black hair.

"Yes, I have" and she pulled back the bedclothes to reveal a swollen ankle..

Sister Riley, the story goes, took one look, stepped closer, smiled, raised her eyebrows and turned to look at the ward, waiting until she knew she had all their attention.

She gave a laugh.

"You're just like a rotten apple!"

Ruth said nothing. She hid her foot under the bedclothes. Fast.

Now the story is doing the rounds today, more evidence of Sister Riley's sadistic streak.

We know, and so does Ruth, that she is too diseased for the drugs to touch and her condition reminds us of our mortality; and we are afraid, very afraid, and hate Sister Riley for reminding us of it.

Chapter 26
Cynthia and the vicar

Vicars are allowed to visit at any time so it happens on one Wednesday afternoon Megan's local minister comes to see her. He is young and good-looking.

Cynthia, the Gwynedd "glamour-puss", drifts in.

"Hello everyone! I've come to have a chat with you."

She is wearing her new white chiffon negligee and she wants to be admired.

Meanwhile Megan's vicar, a single man, gives Cynthia an astonished glance, then drops his eyes and turns a bright red.

He cannot fail to notice her nudity beneath the skimpy bits of material.

"Oh! I didn't know you had company in here," she says.

This is a lie, because the vicar went into her ward first by mistake.

Cynthia smiles at him, the way she does with all men, which

makes him go even redder, then she struts out wiggling her backside, clearly visible beneath the bits of chiffon.

Cynthia's unpopularity lies in her selfishness and her total devotion to her own good looks. Even though she has turned forty, Cynthia is good-looking. She has spent most of her life caring for her face, hair and body and she never misses an opportunity, however small, of parading herself before male eyes for the satisfaction of seeing the pleasure in them.

This does not endear her to other women. Cynthia is married but childless. She keeps a photo of her white poodle on her locker.

After Cynthia walks out, Megan's vicar tries to continue with his account of all that is new in his parish but he no longer seems to have much enthusiasm for the subject. He falters several times and he is so vague over details concerning their recent "bring-and-buy" sale that Megan has to prompt him.

Later in the day Cynthia returns wearing yet another outfit, a white frilly ensemble more suitable for a honeymoon than a hospital.

This time we are ready for her.

"What on earth have you got on?" says Mrs McGrath. "You look like a fairy!"

"Got on? What on earth do you mean? This is just a little present that my husband bought me. He thought I was a bit depressed when he last came in.'

"My, you do look smart," says Bronwen with admiration for she has no illusions about her own beauty, which has long faded, and she has contented herself to settle back into comfortable middle age, long ago. Anyway, her husband likes her like that. "I don't go for those tarted up goods" he once said to her, looking in the direction of Mrs McGrath's empty bed – she had taken to making herself absent at visiting time since she rarely got any and would be found in the recreation room watching "Westerns" on television.

Clothes and the ability to get men are subjects close to Mrs McGrath's heart and her jealousy of Cynthia, endowed with both, is boundless.

"Bloody funny thing to send you in hospital," sniffed Mrs McGrath. "It's more suitable for someone going on honeymoon. He must have got more money than sense."

Mrs McGrath, unlike Bronwen, has not relinquished her hope of a sexual life. Megan and I have yet to begin.

Chapter 27
Mrs McGrath discovers God.

One day, to our surprise, Mrs McGrath expresses a desire to get closer to God, well, to attend the weekly hospital service.

"I'm a Catholic, you know, and I do like to try to keep it up," she says.

This is news to us. I doubt if my former teachers, gentle nuns in their long white gowns, would have recognised Mrs McGrath as a kindred spirit.

A room is kept at the end of the corridor for use as a chapel. All the different Church denominations take it in turns to hold regular services there and when the day approaches for the Catholic service, Mrs McGrath spends a lot of time attending to her hair and make-up. Later she disappears, arm in arm with another Catholic woman from a neighbouring ward.

We watch with amazement at this transformation.

"What do you make of that then?," says Megan, as soon as the door closes.

"I can't believe it," says Bronwen." I had no idea she still practised her religion. Maybe she's had time to think about it since she's been here.'

"Perhaps she wants God's help to get out of here," says Megan.

Mrs McGrath's motives remain unclear. Is it just an insurance policy on her part? Has she faced for the first time, like many of us, our own mortality? Or does she think there is a better selection of men attending the Catholic service than the bingo evening?

Whatever the true reason, she has taken to going to the weekly Catholic service until one day while she is in the process of receiving Holy Communion she had such stabbing pains in her stomach that she has to leave.

She returns to the ward with a nurse trailing behind, holding a glass of medicine.

"Drink this up, it will do you good", says the nurse.

Mrs McGrath sniffs it.

"Bloody peppermint! That won't do me any good at all. I need something stronger."

"I can't give you anything stronger until Sister comes on duty in an hour's time. It's against the rules."

"I want to see a doctor," demands Mrs McGrath.

The nurse shakes her head. "It's against the rules to get a doctor without Sister's permission first."

"But I'm ill. Is that against the rules?"

"You'll have to wait," says the nurse, leaving the phial of peppermint on her bedside locker. Several hours later, a nervous young doctor appears and diagnoses Mrs McGrath with 'grumbling appendicitis', a conclusion she had already reached.

"I don't need a doctor to tell me that."

He puts her on a light diet.

Chapter 28
Bartering

The highlight of our day is the morning post. I'm lucky. Most days I get something.

This morning it's a big box of chocolates from Nellie, a woman who used to call at Ty-Llangenny to buy fresh eggs.

Mrs McGrath gets the occasional get-well-card from some of the regulars in her pub. She did once get a parcel of biscuits bought from the local Co-op with the "special offer" sticker still on it.

She has a son who went away to sea many years ago but she never talks about him.

She is objecting to her restricted diet, for she is a woman who enjoys her food, and, we suspect, her drink.

This, of course, is a most inconvenient time for anyone to be put on a diet, especially a woman like Mrs McGrath. With the Easter weekend upon us there is every hope that the food will be festive.

But Good Friday sees no change to our diet except that we do not get any meat for dinner and we each receive a helping of ice cream for tea.

It's a cold and miserable, with the rain lashing down, and none of us feels like eating it, so Mrs McGrath, ignoring medical advice, tucks into our share.

"I don't care," she says, going from bed to bed collecting the vanilla and strawberry mix.

"Anyway, this is all part of a light diet."

Her violent pains do not re-appear, despite eating three strictly forbidden portions of ice creams. Her mood lifts.

There is just one small problem though.

It's Easter and we all, with the exception of Mrs McGrath, have our beds decorated with Easter cards, outward symbols of our absent friends and relations.

Mrs McGrath sits up in bed contemplating this situation.

The afternoon will bring visitors and Mrs McGrath, aware it will not reflect well on her social status if she is seen to be the only one without Easter cards, casts covetous looks in my direction, the youngest and therefore the most vulnerable, and also the one with the most cards.

"You've got an awful lot of cards."

I say nothing.

"Do you really want so many?"

I know what's coming and I am not going to give them away without at least a bit of a fight.

"Of course I do."

I start re-arranging them so that they look their best for I am very proud of my cards.

Mrs McGrath's voice assumes a firmer tone.

"You haven't got room for them all. They look silly, crammed together. Don't you agree?"

She turns to the other two for support. They ignore her remark, relieved Mrs McGrath's eyes have not strayed in their direction.

"Why don't you give some to me?"

Now, faced with such a bold request I do not have the courage to refuse.

And I have to agree that her bed looks odd without any festive cards. Visitors might think she had no friends.

"Well…"

Sensing my weakness, she leaps out of bed. Within seconds, much to my alarm, she is finguring my cards.

"Come on, let me have some."

"Er..er."

I looked for the smallest, the plainest cards.

"Perhaps I could let you have one or two."

"I want ten," says Mrs McGrath. Her bossy manner quite startles me.

"You're not getting ten. How about four?"

"Six!"

We strike a bargain.

She watches me while I begin to sift through my cards, hoping to pick out six of the least attractive.

"I want some of your decent ones," snaps Mrs McGrath once she realises what I am doing.

"Let me pick my own … how about this big one?"

She snatches an ornate Easter card of Christ, all in white, floating up to heaven.

"You can't have that! The vicar gave it to me and he will be coming in to see me."

This is a lie. My vicar seldom does hospital visiting, particularly to places like Sully, on the grounds that he might catch something, but even Mrs McGrath has to admit she can't take my vicar's card, even for an afternoon. After some negotiation Mrs McGrath is satisfied and retreats to her own bed with seven of my Easter cards, leaving me with eleven.

She sets about arranging them on her bed-rail and later accepts compliments from the women in other wards who stroll in to see what we've got.

Only one suspects the truth: Cynthia.

"Nice to have a lot of friends!" she says staring at the sudden influx of cards above Mrs McGrath's bed.

We say nothing. Ward loyalty forbids it.

Mrs McGrath gives her a fixed smile, holding Cynthia's gaze until she is forced to turn away.

Chapter 29
Celebratory food

All our nerves are edgy today and we bicker away over trivialities.

I had a restless night. Actually I was asleep before ten o clock when the night sister, on her rounds, shone her torch in my face, prodded me awake, and asked:

"Are you all right?" Then walked away. I don't know why.

It was hours before I went back to sleep.

Easter Sunday passed in a flurry of visitors, more presents and more flowers and our spirits lift.

Mrs McGrath keeps less and less to her diet. In the end on Easter Monday, she decides to abandon her light diet altogether.

"That doctor doesn't know what he is talking about. He is only just out of college."

Now Easter Monday is a day of feasting, when food in Sully is said to rival Christmas Day in both its quality and quantity.

Mrs McGrath tells the dietician what she can do with her diet, or rather she tells us what she would like to tell the dietician if she had the temerity to show herself instead of sending instructions via the nursing staff.

Before the dinner trolley reaches our ward, Mrs McGrath walks up and down the corridor several times to ascertain its contents.

She comes back, rubbing her hands together:

"Yummy, yummy, lovely grub coming up."

She has a plan.

"Bronwen, ask for an extra piece of chicken, Megan get extra helpings of vegetables and you Ann ask for extra portions of sauces; all three of them. I counted. And don't forget the stuffing and gravy, just make sure you all get a bit extra."

The trolley rolls in and the staff begins serving our Easter Monday dinner.

"Lovely grub you got there today staff," said Mrs McGrath.

"You're not getting any. Here's yours."

Staff Nurse Evans hands her a plate with some lettuce, a hard-boiled egg, and one tomato.

"I'm not a rabbit," says Mrs McGrath, staring at the plate.

"The dietician is aware of that."

On hearing of our requests for extra large portions the staff congratulate us on our appetites.

"That what we like to see! patients eating plenty!"

Before the trolley has made it to the next ward, Mrs McGrath is out of bed demanding: "what is rightfully mine," her fear of catching the disease forgotten as she is overcome by hunger, not surprising since she has eaten very little, apart from all the ice-cream on Good Friday.

She is so hungry that we have difficulty from stopping her taking some of our own food too.

Megan counts the Brussels sprouts and roast potatoes and even the peas but Mrs McGrath has already scooped up more than her share and is away, ignoring Megan's plaintive cries. I measure out my sauces making sure that they are equally divided though Mrs McGrath, like a cat snatching cream, manages to get an extra portion.

Once Mrs McGrath had made the decision to abandon her diet there was no stopping her for the rest of the day, though we did try to remonstrate with her as she tucked into a packet of cream cakes, a bag of toffee, half a box of chocolates, an orange, some grapes, and even a sausage roll brought in by the afternoon visitors.

At nine o clock, she was still complaining of hunger when she found another packet of biscuits tucked away at the back of her locker.

"It's worms you've got not grumbling appendicitis," said Megan.

Mrs McGrath gave a grunt of contentment.

"Tonight for the first time in four days I can really say I feel full. And happy."

But her stomach did not share her happiness. Two hours after we have fallen asleep, we are woken by Mrs McGrath rushing to the lavatory.

Chapter 30
It's foolish but it is fun

There is a woman in Ward 7 with the strange name of Flicker.

"Why the name?" I ask.

"Because she's always picking her nose and flicking it around," explains Bronwen.

Mrs McGrath is venomous towards her.

"You do know she tells lies, don't you? She spins these stories about the exciting life she has and we all know she works in a bottle plant."

She adds: "And she's downright lazy too. I discovered the other day that she hadn't washed for two days, so I said to her 'It's about time you saw some soap and water isn't it?' We were all in the washroom and she just stood there and watched us. Do you know what she said? 'There does not appear to be much point in washing these days. Wash, wash all the time. I have got better things to do with my time' and she walked out."

Now Mrs McGrath is meticulous about hygiene, and to show her disapproval of Flicker's nasal habits, she arranges for a record to be sent on the hospital record request programme called 'It's Foolish But It's Fun' with the message 'To Flicker. Habits die hard. From an unknown admirer'.

Flicker is not amused and returns the compliment a week later, on hearing the news that Mrs McGrath is constipated, with the record request:

"I try all day but I can't."

Well, this is all very embarrassing, because the truth is that Mrs McGrath does have a problem with this bodily function. It's something to do with her diet and it's the subject of much merriment and gossip.

Women whom we seldom see keep popping in to ask about the state of Mrs McGrath's intestines, and the staff ply her with ever-stronger laxatives.

"How is Mrs. McGrath today? Any luck? No! What a shame! A nasty thing to suffer from is constipation, and it can happen to the best of us if we are not careful."

Talk of this nature does not put Mrs McGrath in a good humour. In the end the pills and potions work, a fact she broadcasts fast and furious throughout Gwynedd.

Chapter 31
Hospital rules and practical jokes

Today got off to a bad start. Catrin, the walking spectre ("you can see straight through her" says Mrs McGrath) and I exchange angry words before breakfast.

I wheeled the mobile phone on its trolley into the bathroom in order to have some privacy.

It's nearly eight o'clock.

Catrin tries the door, finds it bolted and slides back the peep-hole to see me on the phone, and starts shouting about hospital rules:

"Nobody is supposed to use the phone before eight o' clock in the morning…I shall report you to Sister…I want to use the bathroom."

So, after this row I cheer myself up by buying a bottle of red nail varnish off the Red Cross trolley, which comes once a week.

What with three rest hours and four meals a day, I am getting very sleepy and lazy. Last night I was dozing off to sleep when I saw Bronwen creep out of bed and close our window.

"What're you doing?" I murmur.

"I can't sleep with the sound of the sea," she whispers.

That's a lie. It's the fresh air she doesn't like, something I have suspected for some time, despite her years in sanatoriums.

Bronwen seems to be having some kind of a bladder problem. She is forever trotting to the toilet.

No sooner are we settled down to go to sleep of an evening than out of bed she pops again.

She has an easy-going gullible nature and it makes her a natural victim for practical jokes, something both Megan and Mrs McGrath enjoy.

"I wonder if we could talk her into going again?" says Megan.

The idea appeals to Mrs McGrath.

"Let's all talk about water when she returns."

Bronwen, to her surprise, finds us discussing rivers, swimming pools and oceans. Could any of us swim? No, and neither did we know anyone who could.

"I wonder what it feels like to be floating in the sea," murmurs Megan.

"They do say the sea helps to keep you afloat, not like a river or a swimming pool," says Mrs McGrath.

"What a funny subject to talk about!" says Bronwen, sitting on the edge of her bed listening in bewilderment to Megan and Mrs McGrath.

They ignore Bronwen. Instead Megan switches to rainfall.

"I would love to hear a tropical downpour. They say it's very noisy and the rain is warm."

"Listen to the sea tonight."

"It doesn't sound louder than usual," says Bronwen getting into bed.

I like listening to the noise of the sea, ever since that first day I came into Sully. Sometimes it would be calm with the sun glittering on it like diamonds, more often it was a heaving mass of swirling grey water.

All of a sudden Bronwen sits bolt upright in bed.

Half-apologetically she makes her way to the door.

"It's all this talk of water."

"We did it," says Megan, sitting up in bed.

"She isn't the only one whose has to pay a visit," grumbles Mrs McGrath, slipping out of bed.

Megan and I exchange self-congratulatory remarks.

"Fancy allowing yourself to be talked into doing something that you know you don't need to do," Megan says.

Unfortunately we underestimate the power of mind over matter. An hour later, I am still wide-awake while Bronwen and Mrs McGrath are asleep.

I creep out of bed hoping Megan does not hear me.

Some minutes after my return, I am just dozing off when I hear a creak coming from the direction of Megan's bed: she, too, is a victim of her own chatter.

Now that we have discovered Bronwen's gullibility, Megan is on a roll.

Two evenings later she has another idea and voices it when Bronwen has gone to the toilet.

"Let's remove her blankets."

This is a time-honoured practical joke in Sully. Usually they are popped into a wardrobe and the owner soon finds them.

Mrs McGrath has other ideas.

"Hang them outside the window."

Megan leaves the counterpane on the bed and ties the two blankets together, hanging them like an emergency rope outside our window. She places a vase of flowers in front of them.

"There's quiet you all are," says Bronwen on her return.

Silence.

"What are you staring at me for?"

Bronwen peers in the direction of Mrs McGrath in the semi-darkness.

'I'm not."

She is. I can see her little black eyes peeping over the edge of her sheet.

"Why don't you get into bed and go to sleep like everybody else, instead of prancing off to the toilet every half hour?"

True, Bronwen is still having trouble with her bladder.

"I think it's queer that you should all have gone to sleep so early," says Bronwen climbing into bed.

"Aaaah!... My blankets! You've taken my blankets."

She rips back the counterpane to reveal only one of the three statutory blankets.

"You must have made a mistake," says Megan, faking sleepiness in her voice.

"Count again."

Bronwen does. They've gone.

Within seconds, she is out of bed ripping first the blankets off Mrs McGrath's bed.

"Right, just tell me where they are."

The sudden rush of cold night air circulating around her body is almost enough to force Mrs McGrath to confess.

Bronwen makes a grab for my blankets. I hold on tight. So does Megan.

She searches the wardrobes and underneath our beds.

"You must have taken them next door," and she goes into Ward 3.

"Are you planning to escape?" says Cynthia pointing to the blankets dangling out of the window.

Next time Bronwen goes to the toilet she takes her blankets with her.

Confident that she has outwitted us, she puts the blankets back on the bed and leaps in.

'Aaarh!'

She just lands on a bunch of black grapes. Megan's idea.

Chapter 32
The Royal wedding

As a special treat Sister Riley says we can watch the Royal wedding of Princess Margaret to Anthony Armstrong Jones on the television in the women's recreation room for two and half-hours.

The atmosphere is stifling, hot sticky, dark and full of bundled up women, many of them old, coughing into their great grey sputum mugs.

I want to leave.

Some nurses and orderlies have sneaked in.

Through the glass doors I see two young handsome male doctors walk past.

They are engrossed in conversation, talking, laughing. They look foreign.

I look at my companions and hate them, and myself.

Just as the ceremony comes to a climax with the wedding vows about to be exchanged matron enters and orders the staff to return to their duties. They leave in silence.

Sister Riley decides we have had enough entertainment for the day and we are sent back to our beds.

We are annoyed. Yet we dare not say anything. We have sat in that room for two and a half hours in order to see the wedding ceremony and just as it is about to take place we are forbidden to watch.

Returning to our beds we are full of pent-up frustration and we fall to squabbling amongst ourselves. The bickering channels itself into an open argument, discussion would be too polite a word for what ensued. With a sudden animosity that surprises ourselves we air our beliefs.

It's not long before we reach religion.

Without a moment's hesitation I express mine, fresh out of a convent.

Megan squashes me.

"You are nothing but a narrow-minded little prig."

Now I resent this. Had not mother paid a lot of money, well a lot of money for a struggling farmer's wife, to be educated? I have to admit, though, that I am beginning to question many aspects of Catholicism myself.

Megan says: "God is in heaven and the devil below burning in hell and there is the miracle of the world's creation - made in seven days."

I ridicule the idea. "How do you measure time? Where is your proof?"

Megan is silenced. Temporarily. It is her faith. That is all she needs. She believes in it. There is no need for proof.

Megan switches the subject to men.

"If I was married and I no longer loved my husband, I would leave him and go elsewhere."

Mrs McGrath says nothing. Marriage, as far as she is concerned, is something of an open feast.

"Absolute rot!" say I who have never been kissed by a member of the opposite sex.

No matter. It does not stop me having an opinion.

By now we have all fallen out with each other, and it is left to gentle Bronwen to try and bring us together again, for we have to live in this ward, for how long we don't know, months, maybe years.

Our four friendships, forged over the past few months, have been tested today but the necessity of communal living forces us to speak again.

The fall-out from this and many more subsequent discussions is that I begin to question my convent school education. The theories held so dear within the cloistered confines of our school are beginning to shatter when confronted with the reality of the outside world.

Could Sister Philomena have got it wrong?

Chapter 33
The woman who doesn't want to go home

Mrs. Casey from next door pops in to see us. She is middle-aged with long wild semi-grey matted hair, which rarely sees a brush or comb and a grating, almost guttural voice. She is different from the rest because she wears the institution green-striped dressing-gown. Now, there are few women so poor that they have to wear hospital clothes.

Mrs Casey is one of them.

She has never sought to conceal her limited home circumstances, and as for pride, well, she tossed that aside years ago. She has a seventeen-year-old daughter called Gaynor, who was admitted to hospital over a year ago, dangerously ill. It was debateable at the time whether Gaynor would survive. She was so weak and thin that they put her to lie on pillows all the time.

"Neglect on the mother's part," had been written on Gaynor's case file. This bit of information soon circulated the wards and reached Mrs. Casey's own ears. She did not deny it. The maternal instinct was never very strong with her and she says she "never wanted kids," though she lacked the information to do anything about it.

Anyway, Gaynor is now much better, recovered thanks to streptomycin and yesterday she was seen crying for over two hours.

Why? We are about to find out.

"Nice to see you Mrs. Casey," says Bronwen, always the first to welcome visitors to our ward. "You don't come to visit us much these days."

"I don't like visiting," says Mrs. Casey. "I prefer my bed".

Yes, we knew this.

"If I was allowed up for three hours a day, I would be out for walks every afternoon," said Megan with a hint of mischievousness in her voice, for she knows like the rest of us that Mrs. Casey dislikes walks or any form of activity.

"What's that you say? Walks? That bloody Sister Riley says to me 'Have you been out for your half hour of fresh air and exercise today?' So I says to her 'didn't you see me? I waved to you.' The silly bitch! What does she think I am? I would catch pneumonia going out on a damp afternoon like this. It's not right the way they march you outside. It's like a prison."

Nobody says anything

"How's Gaynor?" says Bronwen busy knitting.

At the mention of her daughter Mrs. Casey groans.

"Would you like a cigarette?" Megan proffers a new packet in the direction of Mrs. Casey.

Seeing the cigarettes she moves with surprising alacrity towards Megan's bed and her thin fingers plunge in.

"Thanks very much".

Megan moves the packet away.

"I said one, not half the packet."

Mrs Casey ignores the remark.

She's already got her fingers on two.

"Can I have another?" asks Mrs. Casey. She knows she has got a good story to tell, and she's not going to tell it for less than three cigarettes.

"Go on Megan, let her have another," orders Mrs McGrath, aware of Sully's bartering culture.

Sensing our disapproval if she refuses, Megan lets Mrs. Casey take a third cigarette.

"What happened to Gaynor yesterday?" demands Mrs McGrath. "She was crying for hours."

"It's that sonofabitch Sister Riley! Do you know what she said to the doctors in front of Gaynor and me?"

We can think of many things Sister might say, all of them unpleasant.

"Well, the doctors say that Gaynor can go home."

"Why that's marvellous," says Bronwen. 'When is she going?"

Mrs. Casey groans.

"That's when Sister Riley pipes in and says 'Gaynor Casey can't go home. Her mother does not know how to cook. I doubt if she has ever made dinner in her life!'"

For once, we recognise the truth in Sister Riley's remarks, though it would not have been polite to say so.

"Oh, what a nasty thing to say!" says Bronwen.

"What cheek!" adds Mrs McGrath who, one suspects, is not that strong in the culinary department herself.

"Then what happened?" demands Megan.

"Well, before I had time to reply, the one doctor turns to Gaynor and says 'Where is the nearest fish and chip shop?' Gaynor told him that there was one at the corner of the street. 'That's fine then' he says 'you can go there for your dinner every day. You won't starve on fish and chips' and he just gave Sister Riley a big grin. Of course she, not to be outdone, says 'I suppose Gaynor can go there for her breakfast too?' I could have swiped her one across the face."

She is angry.

"Is Gaynor going home then?" says Megan.

"Oh yes, next Wednesday".

Mrs. Casey is silent.

"I'm going on Monday to get things ready for her."

She smokes her three cigarettes as if they are her last.

For the past nine months Mrs. Casey has enjoyed the warmth, security, and food inside Sully and she would have been content to stay indefinitely.

Instead she is forced to leave, to go back to her damp terraced cottage in Pontypridd with no bathroom, no heating except one coal fire and an outside toilet. Sully, for Mrs Casey, represented untold luxury, one that she could never aspire to in the outside world.

Her husband is disabled from getting coal dust on his lungs, and she has three younger children as well as Gaynor.

Her time in Sully is a welcome break.

Now, much against her will, she is about to be thrust back into her old life.

We are silent. We sympathise with Mrs. Casey. But within a week, both she and Gaynor have gone, never to be heard of again.

Chapter 34
Art in Sully

Before going into Sully I had no interest in art. That was a subject you did if you couldn't handle serious subjects like Latin.

Oh yes, I was an academic snob. So I didn't "do" art.

So the morning Paula, the art occupational therapist came into the ward to introduce herself to me, I dismissed her suggestion that I might like to do some drawing and painting and pointed to my stack of books on my bedside locker. Was I not studying for my A levels? Was I not hoping to go to university? I still nurtured a dream that somehow, somewhere, I might be able to continue my education, though it looked an impossible dream.

Paula persists. So I agree. Next day she brings in a selection of paper and coloured pencils.

I surprise myself. There follows a vast outpouring of drawings, very bad drawings, but I become so immersed in the process

I can't wait for the day to begin so I can draw. My books are forgotten.

As the weeks go by the paintings became more elaborate but there is one recurring motif: a child alone on a mountain.

One day I had just finished a series of drawings again of this solitary child on ever more dangerously high mountain when Paula asks for an explanation.

After all there were no mountains outside, only vast stretches of sea.

Without thinking I say:

"I was in Craig-y-nos".

She nods. "That explains it."

No more is said.

Many years later, after a career in journalism, in my mid 50s, I went to Glasgow School of Art to train as an artist.

And I have to thank Paula, the artist brought in by Sully hospital, for introducing me to the world of drawing and painting.

Chapter 35
Welsh social class system

Friday night is fish pie night, and we are eating it without much enthusiasm the way you do with some food, bland, innocuous, you get it down because you know you have to and there is nothing else to eat anyway.

Bronwen voices our thoughts:

"It's not very tasty is it?" We stop eating.

"You're right," says Megan, putting her knife and fork down. "They've forgotten to put salt and pepper in it."

"Well, I never did like fish," I volunteer, for I am still a fussy eater.

"The food is getting worse," says Mrs McGrath. "I'll be glad to be away from here."

"You started it off," grumbles Megan. "If you hadn't noticed how awful the supper was, I would have eaten it."

The complaints grow until Bronwen, mild gentle Bronwen, suddenly turns and snaps:

"Don't blame me for talking you all out of your supper tonight. You could not have wanted it that badly."

"That's not the point," I grumble, glad of an excuse not to eat my food.

"If you had not suggested it in the first place," adds Megan.

"Shut up moaning the lot of you," says Mrs McGrath.

The prospect of a hungry night ahead has concentrated her mind wonderfully on finding a solution.

"Megan, what have you done with that box of biscuits your aunt brought you last week? It's time you opened it. Ann, where's that box of chocolates?"

"I've got some fruit that needs eating up," Bronwen offers before Mrs McGrath has time to demand it.

I note though that Mrs McGrath's contribution to our impromptu feast is one Swiss roll, which has been in her locker for at least two weeks.

Next day my vicar made one of his rare visits to see me. He told me all about their highly successful jumble sale which made enough money to repair the leak in one of the church windows.

Then he reminisced about "the wonderful people from the mining villages."

He spoke about their warmth and genuine friendliness and I could see the smile getting broader and broader on Bronwen's face.

Only the night before Mrs McGrath, a city person, and Bronwen were quarrelling over this very subject. (Megan comes from the suburbs of Cardiff and that doesn't count: she's neither city nor valley. As for myself, from a farm in the Black

Mountains? Well, I certainly did not count.)

Bronwen complained "city people think themselves superior to us in the valleys." It's true and Mrs McGrath made no attempt to deny it.

"That's not my fault is it?" said Mrs McGrath. "Anyway, it's true."

"But what have you got to be superior about?" said Bronwen.

"Everything," said Mrs McGrath. "Everyone knows it."

Even though she lived in Tiger Bay, an area notorious for its crime and violence, she considered herself socially superior to the rest of us.

Therefore the vicar's remarks came at a most opportune moment. He sat there busy praising the "valley people" while Mrs McGrath glared at him.

As a man of the cloth the vicar failed to realise the social minefield he was treading on.

He added:

"I worked in a mining village for five years, but I'd never go back. It was an interesting experience though not something I'd wish to repeat."

The smiles froze on Bronwen's face while Mrs McGrath, who had been silent until now, smiled and said she quite understood his feelings.

Beautiful, pampered Cynthia from next door is facing the most crucial decision of her life. They want to operate but she dreads the scar it will leave down her back.

She comes in to see us and we are amazed at her changed appearance. The carefully coiffured hair lies flat and her face, without make-up, looks pale and plain.

"You've got bags under your eyes," says Mrs McGrath, a woman not given to tact.

She too is surprised at the sudden change in Cynthia's appearance. Bronwen tries to calm her fears, but it isn't the operation she fears so much as the scar it will leave on her body.

"I won't be able to wear backless evening dresses," sniffs Cynthia into a delicate handkerchief in her hand. Not for her, even in dire distress will she sink to using the big white hospital handkerchiefs.

Bronwen is puzzled, never having worn an evening dress in her life, let alone a backless one.

"But why?"

"I don't want to let my husband down. I won't be able to attend all the social functions in Cardiff."

So that was it. Her husband, a self-made businessman regarded Cynthia as his trophy wife, long before the term was ever coined. It was a status Cynthia relished. Now it was about to be taken away from her, she feared, by an 18-inch slash across her back.

Cynthia is very proud of her tall, smart husband and on visiting days, she would make a point of drawing our attention to him when he drove up in a shiny, big blue car.

Next day, to our utter surprise and amazement, we learn that Cynthia had a 'special chat' with the surgeon, and she is not going to have her lung removed, not even a small portion, after all.

How did she talk her way out of it? Aren't operations necessary?

Chapter 36
A marriage made in Sully

Dorothy's brother, George, is busy courting Brenda from the next ward, and they have secret meetings in the grounds while they are out having their daily half-hour of "fresh air."

This romance started a few weeks ago, with them waving to each other during our early morning tea parties.

"See! There's my brother," Dorothy would say and wave to him.

"What's he like?" asks Brenda.

"Oh not bad…wife died last year."

"TB?"

She nods.

"So he's single?"

"Yes."

"Any kids?"

"Three but his sister is bringing them up."

Brenda digests this information.

"How old is he?"

"42."

"Does he work?"

"No…well he used to…down the mine."

"What does he look like?"

From our ward window he seemed just like another middle-aged dressing-gowned man on the opposite balcony.

"I've got a photo if you want to see."

Well, next day Brenda must have decided she liked the look of the photo because she came in for the early morning tea with a colourful scarf.

"What's that for?" asks Mrs McGrath, a bit suspicious of such flamboyance at half past seven in the morning.

Brenda gives a girlish giggle and casts a look at the window.

There is George standing as usual at the edge of the balcony, waving frantically in our direction.

Brenda lets her tea go cold and stands there for the next five minutes waving her scarf.

And that's how this latest hospital romance started.

Letters follow, records sent to each other over the hospital radio, and both become keen bingo fans in order to spend time in each other's company. Once they have progressed to half hour walks in the grounds, there is no stopping them. They meet twice a week in the bushes.

Still, it comes as a shock when six weeks later Brenda announces she is getting married.

"I've got special permission to leave the hospital for four days," says Brenda on her morning visit.

We are astonished. Mrs McGrath is stunned.

Even by Welsh moral standards this is considered fast. Some women try to put Brenda off but she is having none of it.

George will be her third husband.

"What happened to the others?" demands Mrs McGrath. We have often wondered but dare not ask.

"The first died of TB and the second didn't count."

This strikes me as most odd.

"How can husbands not count?"

Brenda sips her tea, digs into the biscuit tin and leans against the window, scarf in one hand ready to wave to George.

"Well, it's like this…. He was married already but I didn't know it at the time. We had been married for a year when he walked out on me. Then, two months later, this woman turns up at the door to collect a pair of trousers.

"My husband says he left them here," she said. Well, you could have knocked me down with a feather. So I told her she could have the trousers back and the man that went with them with pleasure. He was a right bastard! Nothing but booze, booze and more booze and there I was pregnant with no money."

So Brenda reckons in the eyes of the law that marriage does not count, except she is left with twins to bring up.

Dorothy is thrilled her brother has found happiness and they are going to spend their four-day honeymoon in her home. Brenda has a problem though, as they will be going direct to the registry office from the hospital, so she will not have time to get a wedding outfit.

And so the word went around Gwynedd that Brenda needed some special clothes to get married in.

"I must have something tidy for my own wedding".

Betty in Ward 4 has a navy suit, far too big for her since she lost weight.

"You can have it for £2."

Brenda buys it and brings it in to show us.

The navy suit is two sizes too big.

"It needs to be made smaller," says Bronwen. "Do you want me to alter it?"

"There's kind you are".

Brenda hands it over.

It takes Bronwen three full days working at it for it to fit, if not perfectly, at least comfortably, not that it bothers Brenda who spends little time looking in the mirror.

"I haven't got time to worry about what I look like!" she says "Such a rush decision! I do hope I am doing the right thing."

Gwynedd Ward is seething with the news. Less than two weeks after announcing her marriage, Brenda leaves with George in a special taxi to go to the registry office amidst much cheering, hugging and kissing. She wears Betty's suit altered by Bronwen, and looks quite smart.

And her ward gives her a wedding present of an electric blanket.

Chapter 37
Matrimony and morals

We talk about nothing else but the marriage for the rest of the day.

I am horrified to see matrimony so lightly undertaken, only now I keep these thoughts to myself. I see little point in discussing morals. The folk here don't seem to have any.

Also, it is a subject I am becoming increasingly uncomfortable with myself, as I realise that my own views are changing. Maybe the convent didn't get it right after all.

It is clear Mrs McGrath, Megan and Bronwen envy Brenda her new found happiness. I remain silent.

I find it difficult.

In the end I can bear it no longer and put on my dressing gown to paddle down the long corridor to the singles where Miss Griffiths, spinster and retired teacher, lives.

I feel confident Miss Griffiths will not share the same enthusiasm for Brenda's rapid marriage which everybody else does, but I can not be certain, so I mention the subject in, I hope, a vague way expressing views neither for nor against.

"Did you hear about this morning's marriage?" I ask, a pointless question since the whole of Gwynedd have talked of nothing else.

She thumps her skinny fist down on the bed and sends a pile of knitting patterns hurtling through the air. I bend down to pick them up, feeling quite relieved that for once my judgement of human nature is correct.

"Behaving like a pair of teenagers, and them both in their early forties," says Miss Griffiths.

"That's true," I whisper.

"What might they be going to live on? Love and fresh air? Tell me, do you know how many children they've got?'

I am able to give not only the number of children, seven in total counting Brenda's twins as part of the new family, but also their exact ages, a piece of news which Miss Griffiths had wanted to know for some time.

'Brenda has four, including one set of twins by a man she thought she was married to."

"What do you mean she thought she was married to?" asks Miss Griffiths smelling a whiff of a scandal.

I explain that he was already married, not that Brenda knew it at the time:

"So she says that doesn't count."

On hearing this Miss Griffiths thumped the bedclothes again, sending the Western Mail newspaper up in the air this time.

I retrieve it from the floor.

"She has a boy aged nine, and another girl aged five by her first husband who died of TB six years ago. George has three but his sister is bringing them up after his wife died."

It is clear Miss Griffiths, alone in her room, has given the latest Sully marriage much thought and it only confirms her opinion that the world is morally crumbling.

And I provide a willing pair of ears.

Much later, I return to my own bed with all my religious beliefs and pre-conceived moral ethics juggling in my brain. Now I could not agree with all of Miss Griffiths' views.

Whatever one might say about George and Brenda's behaviour, you could not deny that they were tumbling over with life in all its crazy moods and I liked their spontaneity, their grasping at a bit of love, real or imaginary, and either way did it matter?

Maybe it was Brenda's and George's marriage that again brought the topic of a husbands' faithfulness, or lack of it, up for Mrs McGrath voiced her fears, not for the first time, regarding her husband's enforced celibacy.

"I wonder how he is managing?" says Mrs. McGrath to Bronwen, the only other married woman in the room.

"Yes, I know it's difficult. A week is bad enough, but when it goes into months…" Bronwen dare not finish the sentence off.

"I know, you don't have to tell me," says Mrs McGrath, who suddenly seemed keen on the idea of monogamy. "I wouldn't trust my old man out of my sight. He can't resist a bit of skirt."

"There aren't many men you can," says Bronwen. "But I'll say this for my husband, that I don't have to worry about him there. He's terrified of strange women. Do you know we had been going out together for five years before he proposed? I was his first and only girlfriend."

Mrs McGrath looks at Bronwen in amazement. Is she serious?

"You have got a rare one there. Don't know which is the worst – one that likes them too much or one that likes them too little."

"Oh, I'm not complaining," says Bronwen, quick to defend her shy husband. 'I wouldn't have him different for anything. You see, we're both very much the same – I'm shy with men too."

"Oh Christ! Don't give me that rubbish," snaps Mrs McGrath.

She found it difficult to believe that any woman could be shy with men. Ever since the word go (well, puberty) she had been more than at ease with the opposite sex. "In my opinion, no man is to be trusted after a month away from his wife. How long have you been in here Bronwen?"

"Four months." She is getting cross.

"That's long enough."

Mrs McGrath proceeds to undermine Bronwen's faith in her husband fidelity. In the end Bronwen, who never loses her temper, shouts: "Because you can't trust your old man two minutes out of your sight, does not mean that I can't trust mine, so there."

Megan and I, the single ones, exchange smiles, wondering why these two married women should get so upset.

It is obvious both Bronwen and Mrs McGrath attach great importance to their husbands' faithfulness. Does fidelity really matter? I venture to suggest to Mrs McGrath even pointing out she would know nothing about it anyway.

"Shut your mouth!" snaps Mrs McGrath, as if swatting a passing wasp. "You don't know what you are talking about! All you ever do is read books."

True, but sometimes I do wish Mrs McGrath would apply some logic to her thinking.

Well, details of Brenda and George's wedding reach us on the Gwynedd grapevine and Dorothy comes in to tell us after the weekend visitors. "They had over a hundred guests and they all went back to George's club for the reception," breathed Dorothy, awed at her own lies.

We sniff. Surely she does not expect us to believe that?

"Tell us more," says Megan.

"The wedding went off without a hitch."

"Weddings usually do," replies Megan.

"Well, there were lots of things to eat. You know they had one of these buffet affairs where you all help yourself. Sausage rolls, ham sandwiches, Welsh cakes and even a wedding cake bought from the local bakery that made it especially for them. They had tea and a glass of sherry."

"Who paid for it?" asks Mrs McGrath, the pragmatic one, but Dorothy pretends she did not hear that question.

The next piece of information seems more accurate.

"In the afternoon they had to go to bed because it was their rest hour."

Dorothy is unable to say whether they got up again that day.

Chapter 38
Dentists and babies

Every month, we are required to go to the dentist whether we need treatment or not. This is quite a social occasion, for we have a chance to meet men from other wards and the monthly visit to the dentist becomes the highlight of the day. (Unlike Craig-y-nos where a trip to the dentist was regarded with fear, and quite right too for the man kept a bucket of teeth next to his chair and he was known on more than one occasion to extract the wrong tooth. Such mishaps never happened in Sully.)

A visit to the dentist is one of those rare opportunities when we get to scrutinise those indistinct figures we wave to every morning before breakfast. It's true we do have weekly services in a little chapel at the end of the corridor, but the men who go to the services are not among those who communicate with us from their balconies; sometimes they do go to bingo under pretext of being interested in the game, but the men on the balcony are more likely to be ones that go out for walks, and who knows what might happen in those bushes?

It all happens in the dentist's waiting room if we are lucky.

It was during one of these visits that I got a close look at one of Dorothy's brothers. I thought him good-looking, in a rough kind of way, and report this to the rest of the ward. Mrs McGrath wanted to know his age and I could only hazard a guess "quite old … at least forty" which did not please her, since she celebrated her 42nd birthday only weeks before coming into Sully.

On this particular morning a nurse walks past, carrying a tiny bundle, on her way to the x-ray department.

"Let's see," begs Julie, sitting beside me.

The nurse stops.

"What ward are you from?"

"Gwynedd."

"You're T.B.?"

"Yes!"

"Sorry, this is a heart case," and she walks on.

A few minutes later, another nurse appears with another baby. Julie repeats her plea. We feel sorry for Julie. She's desperate to see and touch babies. Only four weeks before being admitted, she had a baby and now her husband brings the baby along to the visiting room where, against strict instructions to the contrary, she kisses and fondles her newborn son.

"It's a T.B. case," says the nurse.

"So are we."

Julie's arms shoot out to receive the bundle. The nurse gives a quick look over her shoulder, hesitates, almost hands the baby over, and then decides against it.

"Sister might see. I'd get a row."

She walks away and there is an embarrassed silence. We try not to look at Julie. We do not want to see the disappointment in her face.

One man breaks the silence:

"It's a shame when a little thing like that gets it. He hasn't done anybody any harm. With us, it's different. We've only got ourselves to blame. It's the way we've been living."

Nobody challenges him. We accept it.

Is it true? Are we responsible for our disease-wrecked bodies? I find myself wondering how we look to outsiders: another bunch of diseased bodies reared in poverty, to die in poverty.

And it makes me angry. I want to escape Wales, I want to leave all this behind.

But several more years are to go by before I make that train journey to London, armed with a fistful of educational qualifications, my passport to a better world.

As for the social burden of TB, I erased it from my past and nobody knew from my CV about those missing years in Welsh sanatoriums. I became five years younger.

Chapter 39
Home to die

We are just recovering from the excitement of Brenda and George's sudden romance and wedding, when another minor drama happens. Suzie, the tiny 'pocketful of life' woman, has signed herself out.

Her latest gastric has shown that the disease is still rampant and that means at least another year in hospital. The drugs don't work. She says she has had enough. She wants to end her days at home. But the problem is which four walls does Suzie call home? Had not her husband, her third in fifteen years, stopped visiting her ever since he overheard some gossip on the hospital bus about Dr. Serrano catching Suzie and that young man from the men's ward at it in the bushes, and offered them pills to cure their sexual urges.

Suzie knows this, and she doesn't care. Once she has made up her mind to leave, it does not take her long to pack her few possessions and call a taxi.

She comes in to see us.

"I'm going home."

We feign surprise though we already know for such news travels like lightning through Gwynedd.

"Are you sure you are doing the right thing?" says Bronwen with genuine concern in her voice.

Suzie is blunt and unrepentant. "Well, there's no point in my staying here. They told me that if the next gastric was positive, that was it. They could do no more for me, so I reckon I might as well die at home."

"Don't be so morbid."

Mrs McGrath hates any mention of death. "You aren't going to die."

Dorothy joins the small crowd gathered in our ward to say good-bye to Suzie.

She asks what none of us have dared to ask, "Where are you going?"

"Home," says Suzie. There is no mistaking the defiant tone in her voice.

Dorothy strokes her hair then pulls out one strand. "And where might that be?"

"Home."

"But I thought your husband had changed flats?"

"He has. I've got his new address. He is in for a surprise tonight when he opens his front door."

"Let's hope it will be a pleasant surprise," says Megan.

Suddenly Suzie becomes conscious of her matrimonial rights.

"He married me therefore he has got to provide for me legally. If I turn up," she clicks her fingers, "he can't turn me away."

There is an uneasy silence.

She has chosen to forget about her own matrimonial indiscretions and now doesn't seem to be the time to remind her.

Suzie is the first to break the silence.

"Anyway, I've nowhere else to go."

There is a quick communal intake of breath. This is what we suspected.

"You've not seen him for eight months," says Dorothy.

"He might have another woman," says Mrs McGrath, voicing her own secret fears.

"I'll soon find out then, won't I?" says Suzie with that air of desperate confidence that only those who are doomed possess.

She hitches her skirt into place. What little flesh she has left is melting away and the skirt had already been taken in so many times, that it has lost its original shape.

We bid her goodbye. What do you say to someone who is determined to find somewhere, outside of the hospital walls, to die?

"Well," says Bronwen as soon as Suzie had gone, "I don't think she's got much time left."

"Chrissake, shut up!" says Mrs McGrath.

We never did hear what happened to Suzie. Perhaps her husband did take pity on her and forgive those little lapses in the bushes.

Chapter 40
Departure of Mrs McGrath

Good news for Mrs McGrath. She is to go home. Or rather her husband was written to and asked to come to the hospital to see Sister Riley. She told him he could collect his wife the following Wednesday, as if she was some parcel left in a railway station.

Mrs McGrath is both pleased and annoyed.

She wants to know why she had not been informed in the first place. 'Hospital protocol' murmured one nurse, though it's suspected Sister Riley had withheld the information from Mrs McGrath because the two of them dislike each other so much.

Mr. McGrath, the story goes, accepted the news of his wife's discharge without much enthusiasm, a piece of information Sister Riley drops on the Gwynedd grapevine.

"He appears to be very happy living on his own," she murmurs in a conspiratorial whisper to Josie, a nurse known for her love of gossip: "if indeed he is on his own."

And she winks.

Well, of course this got back to Mrs McGrath, and she is furious with Sister Riley but there is nothing she can do about it.

Part of the farewell ritual is the collection of 'keepsakes' from other patients, and Mrs McGrath is determined to get a good supply so she decides to "dress up".

"They are more likely to give, if I do a bit of entertaining first," she says, wrapping her ample form in a supply of sheets, shawls and towels.

"What are you supposed to be?" asked Bronwen. None of us could guess and we were surprised at the answer.

"An Eastern maiden, full of mystery."

"More like an Arab sheik," laughed Megan.

"Shut up…and follow me…you too!" says Mrs McGrath pointing in my direction.

So, we do as we are told, having armed ourselves with empty fruit bowls.

Now if truth were told Mrs McGrath fancies herself as a fortune-teller, an occupation that would have suited her.

Also, the occasion provides her with an excellent opportunity to tell some women exactly what she thinks of them. Predictably, such honesty does not result in an over-generous donation of keepsakes.

It's Megan's and my job to follow her as she tours the beds. One woman puts in a spare set of false teeth. I point this out to Mrs McGrath.

"What do I want with somebody else's false teeth?" she shouts. "Take them back and get something else."

I do as I am told. The woman contributes instead a sheet of writing paper and one envelope: "So that Mrs. McGrath can write and tell us all about her renewed sex life," she says, with a treacherous smile on her face.

"One sheet of paper wouldn't be enough," snaps Mrs McGrath.

It's then that she spots bespectacled, plain Maureen's array of perfume. She keeps her bottles neatly displayed on top of her locker and once a day, she dusts them. Mrs McGrath zooms in with her fortune-telling act.

"You'll marry three times," she promises Maureen, who at twenty-two has never been kissed. Maureen giggles, delighted, and signals for me to approach her bed.

"Do you think Mrs. McGrath would like a bottle of perfume?"

"I'm sure she would."

"Take this one then," says Maureen handing over a half empty bottle of Miss Worth. Mrs McGrath spots this and orders me back to get a "full bottle".

Maureen confides she had not liked the suggestion she would get three husbands "one would be enough".

Wednesday morning arrives. Before Mrs McGrath is awake, two women from Ward 3 creep in and remove her packed suitcase.

The discovery sends Mrs McGrath into such a rage I fear for her heart, and she has not calmed down by the time Mr McGrath, a man who looked as if he had stepped out of a

1930's Chicago gangster movie, comes to collect her.

He pushes the ward door open with his shoulders and did not bother to take his hands out of his pockets.

I would not have liked to have removed any of his possessions.

"What's wrong?"

Mrs McGrath explains. Before she's finished, a face appears in the glass window gesticulating to something outside then disappears.

It is the missing suitcase.

Clearly Ward 3 didn't care for the look of Mr McGrath either.

The "good-byes" are short, for Mr McGrath is in a hurry to get out.

They leave arm in arm for their home in Tiger Bay, an area of Cardiff where you mess with folk at your peril.

We are sorry to see her go. Life is going to be very quiet.

Chapter 41
A visit from the Bible Society

Religion is not a habit you break easily.

So I go to communion in the little chapel at the end of the corridor at half past seven every Sunday morning. This is the last service in which T.B. and non-T.B. patients will be allowed to mix.

It seems the latter have complained about our presence so in future we will have a special day to ourselves.

Now that Mrs McGrath has gone, Dorothy has started to visit us again on a regular basis, to wave to her husband and brothers. She has just told us that her mother was married three times "to the same man." We think it an extraordinary piece of information but Dorothy accepts it as normal.

On Monday we received a visit from the Bible Society, a group of young university students. They talk to us in the little chapel about how they came to be converted.

One young man says that his conversion happened at a mass

meeting. "Suddenly my life had some purpose and I grew to love Our Lord more from that moment on."

I find myself thinking how sweet and innocent they look, how untouched by life, until I realise, with a shock, that they are older than me.

I glance at the gathered crowd of patients, the regular ones, the ones who never miss a service. They are the incurables, who cling to their religion to help them die peacefully, and amongst them is Catrin, clutching her grey sputum mug in one hand and her prayer book in the other. The sight is not a pleasant one and all the while the six students, oblivious to the disease and poverty written on the faces before them, lecture us on God's love for mankind.

I envy these students their easy, untouched lives, lives that have never known the sweet smell of death.

Yet I still believe in God.

Remnants of childhood religion do not drop off overnight, especially those installed in a convent.

Chapter 42
Bombshell

Later that day, we watch a play on television. The hero, a young man, turns to face the cameras with an agonised look on his face. Behind him stands his girlfriend.

"I have something to tell you. I feel it my duty to warn you," he murmurs. We listen. It is rare that a television drama so captures our interest.

"I … I'm suffering from a terrible disease."

"What?" asks the young girl.

"My life is worth nothing," he moans. "I have tuberculosis."

Bronwen, Megan and I snap out of the make-believe world of television drama and laugh. "My life is worth nothing," mimes Megan, stretching herself out in her bed, feigning a death-like posture.

"Ssh! There's more to come," says Bronwen.

"What are the symptoms?" asks the young girl and the man

coughs. This tickles Bronwen. Her years in sanatoriums have taught her how to diagnose the stage of disease by the rattliness of a cough.

"That's the healthiest pair of lungs I have heard all week!" she says.

After this, the play loses its dramatic hold over us and becomes the subject of ridicule.

Anyway, another week drifts by and all the time Mrs McGrath's bed remains empty. We miss her.

Then Sister Riley, on her morning round, announces we can expect a new patient to join us later in the day.

"I wondered how much longer that bed would remain empty," says Megan, after Sister Riley had left the room.

"It's not like the old days" adds Bronwen. "There would have been another one in it before the blankets were cold."

All afternoon we speculate about the new patient. Who would this woman be who would share our lives with?

Would she be young or old? We hope she will be young. Would she be noisy or quiet? Would she love men? We make idle guesses. Towards four o'clock, we hear the lift gates slam shut and the cumbersome rattle of a wheelchair being pushed down the corridor.

"This must be her," says Megan, alarm in her voice.

"Oh no!" groans Bronwen. "At least people can walk in even if they never walk out again. But to arrive in a wheelchair? She must be at death's door."

"We'll have to be quiet".

"And tidy."

"And sympathetic," says Megan. "We'll have to run errands for her, do this, do that. Get me my flannel, pass me my brush and comb … oh no, I can't bear it," says Megan.

With that the door opens and in comes the wheelchair.

With Mrs McGrath.

We shriek, horror-stricken.

What's gone wrong? She looks so ill and pale too. We stare in disbelief. Nothing prepared us for this. We are stunned.

Why weren't we told? Could it be that Sister Riley took pleasure in upsetting us?

Of course, the news travelled fast through the rest of Gwynedd: "Mrs McGrath is back … and so ill too!"

It's some time before we recover and begin to piece together the story behind Mrs McGrath's sudden return to us.

She seems to have got some mysterious illness, which gives her a lot of pain. The only way that she can reduce the pain is to lie flat on her back. One doctor diagnosed a severe drug reaction, though Mrs. McGrath admits there is more to it:

"I was at an all-night party to celebrate my return," she says, "I think I fell down the stairs. But I'm not telling the doctors that. I wasn't drunk…honest to God I wasn't".

We don't believe her.

Anyway, it's like old times having her back and Megan opens a new tin of biscuits to celebrate.

Chapter 43
The mysterious boyfriend

Megan received a letter and spent a long time reading it this morning. She says nothing. This is unusual because letters from the outside world are shared.

"What's wrong?" says Bronwen, always attuned to the emotional temperature of the ward.

"It's my boy-friend."

We stop what we are doing: Bronwen's knitting needles pause mid-air. I put down my book of Keats poems (I feel I have a lot in common with him, well, a shared illness) and Mrs McGrath lowers her copy of the "Daily Mirror".

"You're a dark horse!"

"How come you've never told us about him before?"

"Well, he's not a proper boyfriend."

Still we are impressed. A boyfriend is a boyfriend.

Megan is embarrassed. She doesn't want to talk about him but something in the contents of the letter is forcing her to.

"He's coming to see me this Saturday," she blurts out.

So the story comes tumbling out: "I met him a year ago, on a walking holiday up in the Lake District. Before I came in here, he used to come down once a month to visit me. I have managed until now to put him off visiting me here, but now he says" she re-reads a few lines from the letter, 'I am not taking any more excuses from you, so you can expect to see me this coming Saturday.' What can I do? How can I get rid of him?"

She is desperate.

"Quite simple," says Bronwen. "You write back and tell him that you don't want to see him."

"But that's just what I have been doing for the past couple of months," she says. "It just makes him all the more eager to see me. He thinks I'm playing hard to get."

"What does he look like?" demands Mrs McGrath, never one to turn down a potential suitor.

"He's short and fat with glasses. He works for an insurance company. I think he's a clerk."

Even Mrs McGrath has to acknowledge this is not promising material.

"He keeps writing to me to say he wants to marry me and I keep writing back and saying I don't love him. Then he says 'what difference does that make? I've got a steady job with excellent prospects and I have not got any bad habits. I don't smoke or drink and I have first-class references from all kinds of people.'"

We are amazed. How come Megan has kept this to herself for the past couple of months? Why has she not shared this with us?

"It gets worse. He says he is now almost thirty and he thinks it's time he settled down and had a home and children of his own. But what about me? What about what I might want out of life? All he says to that is that he will give me everything that I want."

"Everything except love," says Bronwen, while Mrs McGrath takes a more pragmatic approach:

"Have you had sex with him?"

"Of course not!' Megan is shocked at the question.

The following Saturday, Jim arrives at two o'clock. He's the first visitor in. Megan's description of him, hardly flattering, does not fully prepare us for the plain looking young man that walks in.

It is clear to us, even myself with no experience, that Jim is not going to light any fires in women's bellies.

Megan introduces him to us while we wait for our own visitors. But he has eyes only for her.

He keeps trying to hold her hand and she pulls it away. Megan is angry. He ignores the signs.

After all, he has travelled all the way from Kendal, up in the Lake District, to see her and he is not going to be put off.

Our own visitors arrive and our attention is taken up with them though I can not help but notice that as the afternoon wears on Megan becomes more agitated. She turns a bright red.

And she runs her hands through her short dark hair until it's sticking up all over, a sure sign she is upset.

"What happened?" says Mrs McGrath as soon as the last visitor has gone.

"I'm livid!" rages Megan. "Do you know what? He's been talking it over with my mother and she told him that I would come to my senses if he waited a bit longer and that I would be glad to marry a respectable man like him! He even went so far as to say that my mother had told him I would not pick up such a steady husband as him again in a hurry and that I'd seen twenty-one come and go a few years ago."

"Well, he can't know much about women to go saying things like that to you," says Mrs McGrath. "He looked to me as if he would be just as dull in bed as out of it." Sexual prowess is Mrs McGrath's main criteria for judging men.

"If you don't like him now," Bronwen says, "I can't see how you can grow to love him. There must be something there in the first place."

I keep quiet. This is a world of which I know nothing, and my time in Sully has taught me there are occasions when it pays to be silent. Very silent.

Instead I watch. And learn.

Chapter 44
The deed is done

I have an x-ray, which livens up the morning, and four days later Dr Davies swishes the curtain around my bed with the news:

"Your x-rays are going up for consultation. You are going to have surgery."

He adds with a smile: "We'll soon get you out of here."

I am relieved.

An operation means I will be out within five months, instead of years.

Suddenly life is looking a lot brighter. (Nearly half a century later while researching "The Children of Craig-y-nos" I discover that by 1960 such operations were no longer necessary for there was an established drug regime by then. But the medical profession still clung to the belief that working class women and children were unable to comply with the long drug regime and an operation was the best option. Anyway, what were highly skilled thoracic surgeons supposed to do? They did in fact transfer their skills and become heart surgeons.)

Sister Riley tells me to ask my mother to come in to sign "the papers".

This is to give permission for a lobotomy, the removal of one lobe in my right lung.

Mother arrives that Saturday afternoon wearing her best navy suit with a white blouse. She looks smart. I walk with her to Sister Riley's office where a team of three men are waiting: the senior surgeon and two younger doctors.

Sister Riley stands, armed folded, watching.

Mother sits down and the surgeon pushes a paper towards her.

She signs. She takes the opportunity to raise questions about my future.

"Will Ann one day be able to work for a living?"

The doctors look surprised, they exchange glances and I feel embarrassed.

Mother persists.

"She was going to go to college before this happened. She was going to be a teacher."

The doctors shake their heads.

"No, she can't do that…far too stressful," says the older man. "Out of the question. She'll never be able to work."

It is mother's turn to show surprise.

"You mean she won't be able to do anything?"

I am angry. What right have these three men, total strangers, to decide what I can or cannot do?

Until this relapse I had been set to become a primary school teacher and had a place in Redlands teachers' training college in Bristol. It was dependent on obtaining a clean bill of health and a clear x-ray.

Well, that didn't happen.

The surgeon glances down at the pile of papers, my notes dating back to my four years in Craig-y-nos, and shuffles them.

"She'll never be strong enough to work…maybe" he looks around the room as if searching for some way out of this embarrassing situation.

"She might be able to do some light office work."

"I don't want to work in an office! I don't want to be a clerk!" I feel like screaming.

Instead I say nothing.

These are doctors. They are in charge. Soon they are going to cut me up. So I keep quiet.

Mother persists. "She was doing her A levels."

At the mention of exams Dr. Serrano, the young Spanish doctor, intervenes: "There's a place in Berkshire…what do they call it? Something for students… Pinewood Rehabilitation Centre for Students."

"Perhaps we could find something out about it," says the other young doctor.

Sister Riley purses her lips into a thin line. The older doctor shrugs.

They make notes.

What exactly is Pinewood, this mysterious place in England, which nobody had ever heard of?

I am excited and alarmed at the same time as I walk back to my bed.

Pinewood, though I did not know it at the time, is to mark the turning point in my life. It offers hope giving me the chance to re-enter the educational system.

Yet I almost slipped through the net, like so many other young people of my age in Wales, who found themselves educationally disadvantaged because of the long periods of missed schooling due to time spent in sanatoriums.

What saved me? A cluster of facts: my mother's determination that I would "make something" of my life, the existence of Pinewood Rehabilitation Unit for Students and a young doctor's knowledge of it.

At my birth, mother set aside a sum of money for me to go to college, it was an insurance policy she took out and every week Mr Howells, "the insurance man," would call at Ty-Llangenny farm to collect this money, and he would get tea, Welsh cakes and fresh eggs at the same time.

Throughout the four long years I spent in Craig-y-nos, where mother never missed the monthly visiting, she still kept paying into this insurance policy, confident that one day I would use it.

Mother had a dream, and she wasn't going to give it up without a fight.

She was determined I would break away from the farm; to a better life than the one she had known.

Chapter 45
Turning point

On a bright June morning Sister Riley stops at the foot of my bed, stares straight at me with her green, cat-like eyes and says: "Thursday".

And moves to the next bed.

I had been expecting it but the perfunctory way in which Sister Riley announces I am to have a chunk of my lung removed takes me a bit by surprise.

I begin packing my belongings for it's unlikely I will return to the same ward after my operation.

Megan has been told that she too will be done the following week and Mrs McGrath is going home at the weekend.

That leaves Bronwen, who faces an uncertain future. Again.

So the preparations begin for major lung surgery, including bathing in disinfectant and shaving under the arms. The anaesthetist arrives to take blood and I am ordered to Sister Riley's office for the procedure. I faint at the sight of my own blood filling a phial, having never fainted in my life before, and return to consciousness lying flat on the floor with a doctor holding my legs in the air.

Later the physiotherapist calls to give me a rehearsal of all the exercises I will have to do.

Suddenly I am caught up in the machinery for a major lung operation and I feel scared. I cry. The physiotherapist takes it calmly.

The next day, swathed in white linen like a corpse, I am wheeled away amid farewells from Megan, Bronwen and Mrs McGrath.

I never see them again.

Passing through the glass doors marked Operation Suite, I am confronted by a chaotic scene.

The painters and decorators are in the process of giving the place its annual overhaul, and the result is that the doctors, surgeons and nurses have to operate in a limited amount of space. A man scratching paint off the floor stands up to make room for us to pass, "Nothing to worry about love," he says waving his metal scraper in the air.

A surgeon saunters by: "Take her to the ante-room." My trolley is wheeled in and I lie there, listening to a group of nurses discusses wedding dresses. One is due to be married in three months' time.

After what seemed like half an hour, a masked, bespectacled man appears:

"Bring her in," he says.

Two nurses push the trolley alongside the high narrow operating table.

"Jump on!" says the bespectacled man, who appears to be in charge. I climb on the table and lie down. Above my head is a large, flat electric light and I seemed to be surrounded by trolleys, covered in green sheets. The window is wide open and I find myself wondering what would happen if a fly or wasp came in. It's a bright sunny June morning and the clock on the operating theatre wall says it's 9.45 am.

At the end of the operating table, a man is busy fixing a cage-like contraption. I dare not think what it's for, so I avert my eyes and look behind instead. I nearly scream! There, less than a few inches from my head, are the thick, gnarled hands of an elderly man, wrestling with a ridged rubber tubular instrument. "I'll be fixing your breathing," he says.

"And I will be helping him," adds another masked, gowned figure.

"Oh, you're the one who passed out on me yesterday, aren't you?"

I nod.

"You don't like me, do you?" he says. I don't care. I neither like nor dislike. He tells the older man about the incident and they both laugh.

"Now," says the young man approaching, "I'm going to give you a big injection."

He starts to rub my right arm energetically, meanwhile talking to his companion. "You want to test my skill as an anaesthetist? Watch this then." He plunges the needle in and I start to count – one, two, three, four … …

I wake up. I find myself regaining consciousness – something must have gone wrong. I am still on the operating table.

"I'm conscious, I'm conscious." The words struggle out over and over again.

"Yes, I know you are," says a nurse at my side.

"What's gone wrong?"

"Nothing. It's all over."

Already? But I had only just gone to sleep. Then I notice the clock.

It's 12.24 p.m. Waves of relief flood through me.

It's over and I am still alive.

"How much blood have I lost?"

The nurse gives a slight jump, for this is not a question she has been asked before by patient lying on the operating table.

She replies calmly, "Not much!"

I had not been prepared for regaining consciousness on the operating table.

Megan is less fortunate, a week later. I hear later on the Gwynedd grapevine she came round while they were still stitching her up.

I am wheeled into a single ward and the next few days are a blur – a hazy memory of drifting alternately between states of consciousness and unconsciousness. And always the pain!

Little had prepared me for that amount of pain.

True, there were injections, yet their effect seemed to wear off within two hours. On the third night, there was a long delay before I received the late night painkilling injection.

Hospital protocol stated that it could only be given after the doctor had made his final visit, only on this particular night the doctor was three hours late. I prayed for strength to bear the pain that was shooting down my back. And nothing happened! I felt cheated. Where was the God that I had prayed to all my life, that I had regularly worshipped?

With a clarity of insight that surprises me, I realise we are alone in this world. My belief in an omnipresent God, ever ready to listen and comfort, is shattered.

What did it all mean? Why was there this craving within us all for some spiritual meaning to our lives, some reason behind the aimlessness of it all?

The night nurse, finally irritated by my persistent 'awkwardness', relents and rings the doctor. She receives the necessary permission and arrives some minutes later with a syringe laden with painkillers.

The following night she warns me: "The doctor is very angry with you. He says a young girl should be able to stand a bit of pain."

But when the doctor arrives, none other than the young Spanish Dr Serrano, he smiles gently, asks if the pain is still there and orders the night nurse to give me another injection. "And something to make her sleep too. I don't think she had a good night last night," he adds.

Chapter 46
Death and departure

Within a week, I am moved out of singles and find myself in Ward 3, the 8-bedder next to my old ward. Usually you get to stay in singles for at least ten days to recuperate before being moved back into the general wards, but my room is needed.

Ruth, the quiet woman with one tooth and long black plait is dying. She must be in her late fifties. We change places. She gets my single room, and I am put in her place in the corner of the eight-bedded ward.

Her husband, Arthur, has been summoned from the pit and the priest called to administer the Last Sacrament.

"I know one woman who had the Last Sacrament three times and she's still alive," says Betty, a woman in her late 30's. Ward 3 is at right angles to the row of single wards, and throughout the day, women come from neighbouring wards to stand and peer through the window at Ruth.

"I wish you lot would stop watching," says Betty. "She's got a right to die in peace, without you lot all staring at her."

Other women back her up.

"If I was dying, I wouldn't like to think you were all standing there watching me go."

"There's such a thing as decency," says Kate, a quiet, sensible middle-aged woman getting out of bed and placing a large bowl of flowers in the window, thus obscuring the view of Ruth.

Night arrives, my first in the ward, and I am surprised by the sudden burst of activity.

"What's going on?"

Jean, a twenty year old, is going from bed to bed, carrying a large shopping bag. Women are dropping food into it.

"Have you got anything you don't want?" she stops by my bed.

"No … no!" Fresh out of singles and still recovering from the operation, with my possessions all in a bit of disarray, I have yet to sort myself out.

"Come off it! You don't need all those grapes and bananas."

She helps herself to my fruit bowl.

"What's it for?"

"Nancy and Maggie! We bribe them to give us hot water to make tea. You do want tea, don't you?"

"Yes, of course."

We had long suspected strange goings-on in Ward 3 late at night, though it never occurred to us it was tea parties organised in a secret deal with the night staff.

Everybody contributed, indeed it would have been difficult not to, and Jean marched with the night's offering into the kitchen.

We hear screams of delight and laughter as the two night staff examine the contents of Jean's voluminous shopping bag. She returns a few minutes later with a large jug of hot water.

We drink the tea and eat our biscuits. Suddenly Cynthia, the beautiful, childless, middle-aged woman who had refused surgery on the grounds it would scar her body, points to Ruth.

The flowers had been removed for the night and now we see Dr Serrano and the priest standing beside her. Arthur, her husband, sits holding her hand.

"She's dying", says Cynthia, excitement in her voice. "She's dying."

We stop drinking tea. We watch, as if hypnotised, feeling both guilty and ashamed. After all, it's Ruth dying. Only the day before, her bed had occupied the space that mine is now in.

The doctor watches her. She shudders, blinks, then her head drops to the left. It's over.

Dr Serrano, who had given me the painkillers a few nights before, bent down and felt her pulse. Her husband covers his face and his shoulders shake with weeping.

"She's dead," says Cynthia, the first one to break the awkward, terrified silence. Even she is humbled, watching the last few minutes of another human being.

Next morning, the bed is empty.

Some weeks later, during the morning round, Sister Riley

stops at the foot of my bed.

"You are being sent to a Student Rehabilitation Centre in Berkshire."

She turns and walks away offering no further explanation.

What's a Student Rehabilitation Centre? Where's Berkshire? The questions tumble out except there is no one to answer them.

On the 26th August 1960, six weeks after the death of Ruth, I leave Sully for England.

I am 18 years of age.

Epilogue:
Pinewood Student Rehabilitation Centre, Wokingham, Berkshire

"Chance is always powerful. Let your hook be always cast; in the pool where you least expect it, there will be a fish."
Ovid

It was that chance remark by Dr Serrano in Sully that got me back into the educational system, and I went on to become a journalist. Unlike many people of my age and background, I had not slipped through the educational net.

Pinewood Student Rehabilitation centre in Berkshire was set up in 1952 to enable students to continue with their studies while they still received treatment for TB.

Technically it was for university students or lecturers, but they had provision for people who did not fulfil this criteria, like myself, six months short of becoming a full time student for I had already been offered a place at a teachers' training college in Bristol.

The Health Year Book 1955 explains: "The British University does not make freedom from tuberculosis a condition of acceptance. The student is x-rayed after he has been awarded a place and, if found to be tuberculous, can then submit himself for treatment confident in knowing that he can return to his studies when he is fit and well again.

Medical treatment of the tuberculous student is the same as that of any other young patient. Socially, however, there is one great difference. A student can do useful work while still under treatment."

Ever since 1930, student organizations in England had been trying to start an institution where tuberculosis students could continue with their studies.

But it was not until 1952 that a 16-bed Rehabilitation Unit was established at Pinewood Hospital, offering a combination of lectures and tutorials.

It became my lifeline.

On arriving at the centre, I was taken to a bright airy second floor flat overlooking pine forests, and given my own room in the women's unit.

We were a collection of fifteen students mainly from India and the Far East. I was the only one from Wales.

Looking back to those far off years I try to relive my immediate impression. All I remember is the surprise and delight that we are treated with respect by members of the staff, that we have a comfortable sitting-room with a record player and stacks of records, something I had never seen before.

It was here that I discovered a love of classical music.

Within days of my arrival a whole team of tutors are lined up to give me individual tuition for my A levels: a Latin master from Wellington boys public school - a prestigious school only a few miles away, Dr Davies from London University in geography and a woman historian again from London University.

One occasion stands out. Dr Grant, the head doctor, sat down and ate lunch with us. (Already I have learnt to call this midday meal lunch not dinner like in Wales). What's more it's one cooked by another student patient, a Sri Lankan girl. Is he not afraid of catching something from us?

It was the first time I had ever encountered a doctor who listened to us. Suddenly we felt we mattered, we were no longer just numbers, just diseased bodies. He asked questions about our lives and listened to what we had to say.

I remember him telling me that they had a copy of Richard Burton reading "Under Milkwood" in the Unit, and I tell him I had already found it.

He seemed genuinely interested in our welfare. We were no longer just numbers.

Pinewood had none of my Welsh baggage, the claustrophobia of rural farm life, or those secret shameful years hidden away in Craig-y-nos Castle as a child or the close proximity with death and poverty in Sully.

Here in Pinewood, set appropriately enough in acres of pine forest in Berkshire, a few miles from Wokingham and its more notorious neighbour, Broadmoor Prison, life took on an air of optimism.

Thanks to the Almoner, a social worker affiliated to the hospital, I found myself slotted back into the educational system and I went on to do my A-levels in Cardiff Technical College.

Finally life normal life begins, thanks to my mother's determination, a chance remark by a young doctor and the existence of Pinewood Rehabilitation Unit.

Pinewood had offered me a glimpse of another world, one I could aspire to despite the childhood setback of TB.

Most of the other students were from Third World countries and already familiar with the ravages of TB .

Yet they were the lucky ones. They were diagnosed while studying in England and are getting treated. At home they would have died.

And I too have escaped. I leave behind Wales, a country obsessed with the past, a country summed up by the poet RS Thomas: "sick at heart worrying like a dog with a bone."

It is 1960. The future beckons.

Part Two
Patients and staff stories

1930s

STAFF

Clara Gould OBE- first matron of Sully, 1936-1950

As a small child Clara had a dream. She wanted to be a nurse.

But it seemed impossible. After all, she was the eldest of 14 children born into a poverty-stricken family in Ipswich, Suffolk in 1886.

Yet she went on to become the first matron at Sully, a great pioneering hospital, and was later awarded an OBE for her services to nursing.

Her story is a remarkable one, and one almost lost, of a woman who gave her whole life to the services of others.

Her great niece, Jill White, now living in Ipswich, tells her story:

"Clara got a job as a maid in Ipswich hospital before going to

London in 1922 to train as a nurse.

After working in London for a number of years the opportunity arose for her to become the first matron of Sully in 1936.

It was a groundbreaking appointment and one that she embraced with tremendous enthusiasm.

She was to remain there until 1950.

"Sully became her life and she loved her fifteen years there," said Jill.

"She used to travel back to Ipswich in her little yellow car to visit her mother and family. This was in the days before the Severn Bridge.

"She had a flat in the nurses' quarters of Sully. Because she never married, her family were very important to her, and she was the one who kept in touch with everyone."

When she retired, she thought of getting her own flat but was advised against it by family members on the grounds that she was not in the least domesticated. All her life she had people to cook and clean for her, having always lived in nurses' quarters. So she moved into an apartment in a hotel in Surrey.

For her leaving presents, she was given a silver tea service and a wealth of other presents, which Jill now has in her keeping.

Clara collected spoons. "Whenever people went on holiday they would bring her back a spoon," says Jill, who now has that collection in her safekeeping.

Her retirement coincided with the introduction of the life-saving drug, streptomycin.

Jill White, her great niece, said her aunt was totally devoted to nursing and never married, though she often spoke with great affection about "Teddy" who worked at Sully hospital.

The family never met him but they think he was a doctor.

Jill said: "My great aunt thought he was out of her social class and that she was not good enough for him."

"Aunt Clara used to dress me up in her uniform after she retired. I was only about six years of age at the time. I think it inspired me to become a nurse," says Jill, who recently retired after a career in nursing.

Clara Gould was a modest gentle woman. She died in 1965 having been awarded an OBE for her services.

Student nurse Iris Deli – Most were terminal cases

Sully Hospital was a place of great hope for so many patients and their families in 1936.

It promised an alternative and more humane method of dealing with TB, in contrast to the traditional strict harsh sanatorium regime. Nevertheless, until the invention of streptomycin there was no cure apart from bedrest and food, and it earned the reputation of being a place for "no-hopers," a place you were sent to die.

Iris Deli was an 18-year-old student nurse in 1936. She recalls her interview with Matron Gould: "She was a lovely lady and I had the greatest of respect for her.

"After some initial training, I was assigned to a ward where the patients were all young girls in their teens that had come from Glan Ely hospital.

It must have been wonderful for them to come to such a lovely place.

Although most of them were terminal cases, there was always hope and they were the happiest girls I had ever met.

I nursed a girl who had been in my class at in Gladstone Road School, and, until recently, was an active member of the WRVS.

We worked long hours with split shifts, during which we had to attend lectures and had little remuneration – 19 shillings a month, but we were happy and contented in the fact that we were, to the best of our ability, trying to make life a little bit more comfortable for those more uncomfortable than ourselves.

I worked there for three and a half years, and kept in touch with many nurses for years afterwards.

Some of the happiest years of my life were spent there."

1940s

STAFF - DOCTORS

Dr Len West – Science is measurement

Dr Len West played a pivotal role in pioneering medical research at Sully.

Thirty years of living in Britain did not change the Australian characteristics of Len West. He was enterprising, competent and interested in science to an extraordinary degree.

"Science is measurement" was his motto and he never fell short of it, whether it was in building the first tomography apparatus at Midhurst, or making the equipment for and performing the first cardiac catheterization in Wales.

Constructing highly sophisticated electronic apparatus for clinical and research investigations were among the many activities at which he excelled, and undoubtedly it was he who laid the foundations of specialized cardio-thoracic work in Wales.

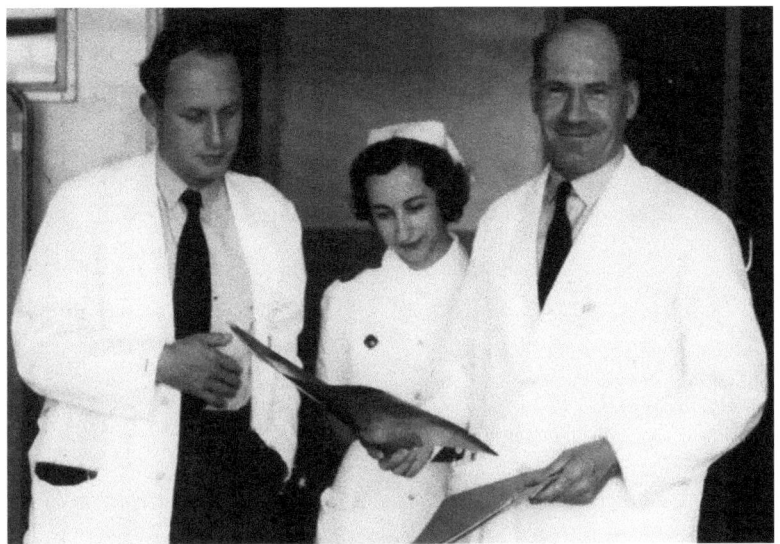

Hugh Richmond (left) with nurse and Dr Len West

In addition he was a good teacher and lecturer as well as a sound clinician.

Len West will be well remembered by his many friends for his impish humour, for his bravery, which was exemplified during his long and painful illness, and for his outstanding ability as a chest physician, scientist and engineer.

"He was at Sully from 1948 until his death in 1970 from lung cancer," said Rosie his daughter. "Sadly he was only 59 years of age. Like so many doctors of that time he smoked."

She remembers attending many children's parties at Sully on Saturdays accompanying him to the hospital.

The following obituary appeared in the British Medical Journal on 15 August 1970.

"Dr.L.R. West, consultant chest physician, Sully hospital,

Penarth, Glamorgan, died on 11 July at the age of 59.

Leonard Roy West, a South Australian from a medical family, was born on 20 May 1911.

He received his medical education at Adelaide University, graduating M.B., B.S in 1935.

After some jobs in Adelaide he came to London to work for his M.R.C.P, which he took in 1937.

He had house physician posts at the Brompton Hospital and King Edward VII Sanatorium in Midhurst before enlisting in the R.A.M.C in 1941.

During his military service he was in Gibraltar, and joined the 6th Airborne Division, which landed in France on D-Day. At the crossing of the Rhine he was mentioned in dispatches,

After demobilization he went back to Midhurst and in 1947 was appointed chest physician to Sully Hospital, to which he devoted the rest of his life.

He was a member of many learned societies including the Thoracic Society and the Cardiac Society, and he was elected F.R.C.P. in 1967.

His memory will extend far outside the immediate area of his work through the many graduates from all parts of the world that he instructed.

He leaves a wife and a son and a daughter."

> Dr. LEONARD WEST
> M.B.B.S. Adelaide; F.R.C.P. London
> 1911 – 1970
> PLANNED AND DEVELOPED
> THIS RESEARCH LABORATORY
> AND IT IS NAMED IN HIS MEMORY

1950s

PATIENTS' STORIES

Poems written by TB patients, 1953, in the Flotsam magazine

Men knitting and communal singing are among the images that emerge from poems published in Flotsam, the Coronation issue of the hospital magazine.

They offer a rare insight into life inside Sully from the patient's perspective. While the men talk of "the bug" and can't wait to get home, the women are more resigned.

Overall what comes through is their camaraderie and sheer optimism even though many would die.

Janet Richards from Llanwit Major said:

"My mother, Clara, was in Morgannwg ward G for many months and she is mentioned in this poem. She was one of the patients selected for the streptomycin trials. She once told me they were the "No hopers".

But thanks to this miracle drug my mother survived."

Here is a selection of their poems:

Women's Wards

"G" Ward
In Morgannwg ward "G"
Four young women you'll see.
Two of them doing their postures.
Though they lie on their sides,
To rules they abide,
And never lie on their Posteriors.
The two young women, namely Olive and Iris,
Have done their postures before,
On Olive's two hours, she arranges the flowers,
While Iris is up for the four.
But for Margaret and Clara,
They are the sad pair sir,
 They put not their feet on the floor,
But they both have to stick it,
And even perhaps like it,
Although their bottoms get sore.

"D" Ward
Morgannwg "D" sees four new cases,
Quite a change from the babies' faces.

First comes Ida. She's the oldest
And we think she is the boldest.
Asking doctor what she's got,
Doctor says - "T.B. you clot!"

Next comes Ruth, engrossed in knitting,
She wishes she could do some spitting.
As it is, she has a gastric,
But there, - that's not so very drastic.
Third comes Ann with her big feet
Hoping she won't rip the sheet.
In the ward are ants galore
But her hoofs will kill them by the score.

Avril then comes last of all.
She used to lie facing the wall.
But now she's moved to the other side,
And watches the ships ride side by side.

Morgannwg Ward

"A" Ward
Morgannwg nursery has eight little girls,
They are precious as eight little pearls,
They look so angelic asleep in the night,
But at five in the morn, they shout with delight.
All day they are happy, their laughs cheer the ward.
It's just like a tonic to one who is bored.
At the end of the day their sleepy eyes close,
Those eight little girls in sweet slumber repose.

"F" Ward
Here they are in "F"ward,
Funny faces-Four!
Letty, Margaret, Eunice,
Katie near the door.

They are neat and peaceful, Loving gentle jokes.
Placid, their enjoyments,
Knitting, sewing, books.
If they could but wander on the garden path,
They would go beyond the Sully Hospital
Meanwhile four do wonder,
Wait, and lie and - —

"H" Ward
On the right is Dilys Price,
Though she is quiet, she is very nice.
Cynthia is next, she is quite new.
She is very cheerful, and likes our view.
Then there is Gretchen, from Pied Piper town,
She came in half dead, but she soon came around.
Last there is Gladys, she just had BI.
And longing to go home to her husband and son.

"G" Ward
When you come into Dyfed G,
These are the girls whom you will see.
Marion on posture is our crossword girl,
She does so many her head's in a whirl.
Betty from Swansea is our football fan,
To win a few thousand is her future plan.
Little Alice, just four feet and a dot,
Thinks that she's taller but really she's not.
Betty, her op over and on the mend,
Soon to Pontardawe her way will wend.
Our rhyme now over we say Au Revoir,
And wish you good health who ever you are.

"H" Ward
We open the door to Dyfed H,
And this is what we would like to relate.
First comes Gwyneth, a buxom lass,
She's signed for her op. but can't take P.A.S.
Next comes Glenys, who looks so forlorn,
That all she thinks of is going home.
Then there is Dorothy, who thinks she's a singer,
We all agree it's not bad for a beginner.
Last comes Sylvia from Penrhiwceiber
She's on the new drug and hopes it will revive her.

Gywnedd Ward
"Good morning, Sister, on this great day,"
Said the nine beautiful damsels of Ward A.
We will be good, if you will only say,
No injections, Cascara or P.A.S Just be gay.
Iris may eat to her heart's content,
Bronwen is grateful for wool you lent,
Pat's smiling face is sheer delight,
Beryl may serenade Doctor tonight.
Minnie's face is burned brown one side,
Doreen is soon to go for a ride.
Alma is anxiously waiting to wed,
Hilda is the one who looks charming in blue,
Evelyn is last and we are proud to say,
Will present Gwynedd Ward with a son one day.

"B" Ward
Betty is our baby, Oh! what a girl,
 We are trying to teach her plain and purl,
But she is busy dreaming of Farley Granger,

Each day her garment gets stranger and stranger.
Joanna is the one who likes to sing,
She's always flying on broken wings,
She like music by Brahms and Schubert,
Ad she simply adores someone called Hubert.
Mary's our darling so kind and sweet,
She says every morning "Come on girls, Eat!"
Next week she hopes to have her Op.
When she gets well she'll make things pop,
Lily likes opera and ballet,
And any orchestra especially the Halle
At the moment she's up in the stars,
Flying with Dennis Wheatley to Mars.

"D" Ward
Now Sister's collected the bottles in,
Betty lies a-shivering.

Olga, a new patient, has been here a week,
We hope her stay will be short and sweet.

"E" Ward
Open the portals of our Ward "E",
Fling wide the doors and you will see.
A bevy of "Beauties," One, two and three,
Gently sipping their morning tea.
First there's Edna, our oldest hand
Of witty tongue- a mimic grand.
She's corresponding every day,
We can't think what she has to say.

Hazel, Tess, Ernestine,
Favours the "Wearing O' The Green."
At wandering she beats us all,
On "Newportonians," she loves to call.
Elsie Beryl is a mother of five,
She could certainly do with a brand new "hive".
Knitting busily from morn till night,
To clothe them all once they're in sight.
Irene has a tiny son,
She hopes he will remain as "One,"
These days she's suffering from "The blue"
Or some such chemical of similar hue!
The baby of the ward is Meg,
She fancies the size of her arm and leg!
Each morning she is like a lark,
But sleeps each night before it's dark.
Hilda hails from Newport too,
We rarely find her "Without a clue".
Of course she longs for hearth and home,
We hope no more she has to roam.
May keeps trotting back and fore,
She's wearing out the old ward floor.
Soon she'll be on her way from here,
Back with all she holds most dear.

"F" Ward
Sully's a beautiful place (they say)
But, Beryl and Blanche, Joan and May,
Want to go home; that's their decision
In spite of the fete and the television.

Men's wards

Powys Ward

"C" Ward
Dick in the corner is on a diet,
Eric stops singing and everything's quiet.
Norman looks at P.A.S with eyes full of hate,
John lies there moaning, "The mail ain't half late."

"D" Ward
Here in this ward, without a doubt,
We consider ourselves the odd men out.
First there is Danny whose main pleasure
Is reading the comics in his hours of leisure.
Then comes Dick, with embroidery supreme,
The articles he sews are fit for a queen.
Opposite is Ron with the deafening voice,
We don't want to hear him, but we have no choice.
The fourth of our party is Vic so "bright"
Dozes all day then can't sleep in the night.
We are happy enough for our ops. are o'er
Good luck to the others who dwell on this floor.

"E" Ward
In first bed left we have Don "Juan" Giles,
To win fair hearts he uses his wiles.
Then comes Bill Davies, Gerry Tuck and Charles Vaughan,
A trio like this should never have been born.
Next comes a bloke, who's a quarter of a penny,

We leave Hugh Farthing and go to Cliff Bevan,
Who honestly thinks that Sully is heaven.
But young Tommy Roach has a different view,
For his consultations are long overdue.

Then last Peter Sellick a promising lad,
He talks quite a lot but is never sad.

"G" Ward
First there is Bill of nautical fame,
Whose present condition the "bug" is to blame.
Next we have Allan, just down from Talgarth,
Who shows Fred delight in that rare occupation of knitting a scarf.
He claims if not used, it will keep the bug warm.

Last of all is Bryn whose
departure is soon. We wish him God speed when the day does arrive, and I know he'll be happy from the bug he's survived.

"H" Ward
There's Glyn from the Mardy who was recently wed,
Then the bug came along and plucked him from his bed.

Barth Ward
In "A" ward there are patients nine,
They have no women, nor any wine,
But sing, they can, and all day long,
They enchant the air with merry song.
Vince, Trevor, Terry and "How",

Sometimes sing when having their "chow".
Jerry, Dan. Cyril and Jack,
And even Prior, they all have a crack.
My, Oh My, did I say merry song,
They've started again, I guess I was wrong.

"B" Ward

Four Sully patients settled by the sea
One's name is Bill that leaves three.
Three Sully patients, operations through,
Tom comes from Hereford, now for the other two.
Test-match fan Bill cheers every England run,
In which he is supported by Phil, the remaining one.
Four Sully patients settled by the foam,
Won't be awfully sorry when they leave for home.

"D" Ward

Now we stroll into Barth Ward "D"
Four boys from Monmouthshire you'll see.
First comes Brian with his guitar.
Who serenades us from afar.
Next comes Dave who is so stout,
"Seconds." is his favourite shout.
Operations! Bill's been through it,
First part Thora, "Nuffink to it,"
Donald comes from up the hills,
They keep on feeding him on pills.

"G" Ward

In "G" we have Ted,
A bus driver was he,

Spends all his spare time,
Drinking cups of tea.
Next we have Trevor, who is a real terror,
Especially when showing the staff how to measure.
Then we have Bill, a cool customer is he,
Who hasn't time for this new fangled TV
Lastly comes Doug, and he's on B.3.
Waiting patiently for the day when he'll be free.

"H" Ward

Len Graham, just arrived at Sully,
Gazes out upon the sea.
Asks himself that well worn question,
"Just how long here will I be?"

PATIENTS

Joyce Jones (nee Cole) – I found a wreath on my chest.

Joyce, age 83, says:
"I remember the shock I had when I came around from my operation to find a wreath on my chest. I thought I had died!"

A young nurse happened to be carrying a wreath when she heard ward Sister Cole call out to her and she was in such a hurry to answer that she dropped the wreath on the nearest bed she was passing.

"The poor nurse got an awful row from sister and I felt sorry for her."

"I must admit though it did give a fright. I thought I had died and passed over to the other side."

"I still have very vivid memories of my time spent in Sully from 1951-53. I come originally from Tredegar but now live with my daughter in Sussex.

"Every bed had a sea view. It was an amazing building," said Joyce, who was taken ill just before her twenty-first birthday.

During her two years there she had two partial lobotomies, (removal of a lobe from each lung.)

She remembers the beautiful grounds but never got to walk outside during her two years there.

"The first 18 months were spent in bed."

She had streptomycin and PAS, still relatively new. The first trial of the drug took place in 1948 in the UK, and Sully was one of the hospitals chosen for the study.

"I vomited my heart out every other day- always at night. I can still recall the taste of PAS."

She has fond memories of the staff in Sully, in particular a young German nurse called Gerda who later visited her at her home in Tredegar.

Each Christmas, the wards would select a representative to go into Cardiff to do their Christmas shopping.

"Well, I was asked to do it one year just before I left and I was so thrilled. But Sister stopped me. She said I was not fit enough. I was so disappointed."

"On Christmas Day, the surgeon, Mr. Dillwyn Thomas, carved the turkey. We had a great time."

"I remember how men and women were kept segregated. I never heard of them mixing, except once when we had some famous cricketers come in to talk to us, and we were all allowed to mix in the recreation room. That is the only time I recall."

"But then you did not even mix with women from other wards."

(Strict segregation between wards was part of the national policy at the time for treating TB patients for fear of cross-infection.)

Joyce recalls the incident when one patient, fed up with not getting "seconds" of chips because the staff kept them for themselves, got hold of a packet of sugar and sneaked into the kitchen after the trolley had finished its rounds of the wards, and poured sugar on them.

They got their "seconds" after that.

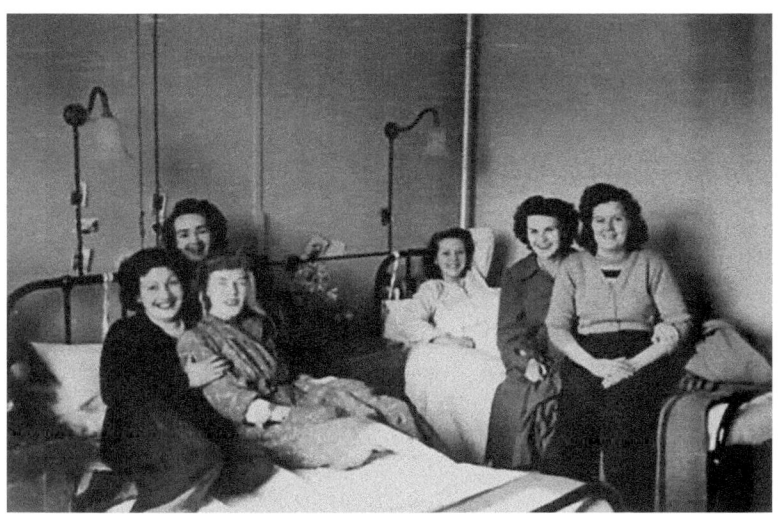

Inside Sully ward, early 1950s, (from left to right) Betty from Swansea, Naomi Llewellyn Seven Sisters, Neath. Cynthia Klase, Pontllanfraith, married to an American, Ella who died at Sully and Joyce Cole, from Tredegar now living in Sussex and Jennifer.

Photo Courtesy Joyce Jones

"The food was not awfully good though there was plenty of it. I used to get an uncle to bring in a flask full of bacon, sausages and tinned tomatoes and I would share it out with the others in the ward afterwards."

Joyce remembers Ella from Ammanford who shared her four-bedded ward.

"She never came back from her operation and her name was never mentioned again.

"A few of us asked what had happened to her but the staff would not say."

We had visiting every weekend.

On Saturdays, my parents would take the bus from Tredegar and on Sundays, Pryce, my boyfriend made the weekly journey to Sully. He wrote to me every day throughout my two years there, except on Sundays.

"Once during some very bad snow, he left the house in Tredegar at 9 o'clock in the morning to get the bus, but it broke down in the snow and he didn't get into Sully until the bell was ringing for visitors to leave.

He asked for special permission to pop up to the ward to say "Hello" to me.

But permission was refused. He did not get home until after 10 o'clock that night."

Joyce and Pryce did marry after she came out of Sully, and five years later their daughter Elizabeth was born.

"I remember being told not to breast-feed her".

They enjoyed 52 years of happy marriage until his death a few years ago.

Joyce's health is not too good these days, for she suffers from severe rheumatoid arthritis.

But her laptop offers her a window to the outside world and a link to memories of a by-gone age.

Alan Workman: TB and heart patients forbidden to mix.

"I live in Australia, been here 40 years, and getting on a bit now but still good.

I was a patient in Sully for about 3 months, in the chest surgical ward downstairs. We were not allowed to mix with the other patients, but used to communicate with them by holding an orange in one hand and writing in the air in big letters.

I had part of my lung removed, a major op in those days, but I am now 80 years of age and still going strong."

Tony Hooper: It would have made a great resort hotel!

"I was an inmate at Highland Moors, near Llandrindod Wells, from 1947-48, and I remember it with no affection at all," says Tony Hooper from his home in Bath.

"At age 7 to be called by a number (No 20 in my case) was not a pleasant childhood memory- the winter of 1947 up there was very harsh.

"The food -I realise it was just after the war- was grim even by standards of the time - bread and marge - or bread and jam for tea (never bread + marge + jam!) - The odd times my parents on their monthly visit managed to find a few fresh eggs from a farmer on the way as a treat resulted in my getting scrambled eggs at the next meal - made from powdered egg! The staff claimed the eggs got broken on the way to the kitchen. This was the standard excuse.

"In the time I was there I lost nearly a stone in weight.

A few years later I was an inpatient at Sully several times- this would have been 1952-1954. A completely different experience- good food, caring staff and a wonderful situation- it would have made a great resort hotel!

Did it affect me? That's a hard one. I guess all experiences feed in to one's personality but I can't say that it traumatised me- though the level of harshness and impersonal relationships with staff made me very keen to be at home when possible. So I was never one for after school activities etc."

Philip Cox: How they kept children in bed

"In Craig-y-nos they tied you to the bed. In Sully if you got out of bed and you weren't supposed to, then they took your pyjamas trousers off you. I hated that!"

He went into Craig-y-nos in 1953 as a three and a half year old and later transferred to Sully for a lung operation.

Despite his poor start in life he went on to become a rugby champion in school and won numerous medals for sport including throwing the javelin.

Philip lives in Pontypool with his family.

Margaret Smith – experimental heart surgery

Margaret Smith, a former child heart patient from 1956, was admitted to the hospital as a four-year-old.

"I was suffering from Ebsteins Syndrome, a congenital heart defect.

"It is now thought it could have been linked to my mother, who suffered from post natal depression, and had been given lithium during her pregnancy."

Born in Pontypridd, her parents had a long journey from the family home to visit her, which involved taking two buses, and her father had to take a day off work.

One day on visiting they got told they could take Margaret home.

"I remember running up to them in just my knickers and vest because I had no clothes. These were all taken off you and sent back home when you were admitted."

"So they wrapped me up in a blanket and I went home - on two buses! It was either that or my parents having to make another long journey to get me. We had no telephone in those days.

Her memories of Sully are happy.

"I was only there for a couple of weeks but I remember it as a cheerful, sunny place where we could go out and play in the garden."

The test of whether she was fit enough to go home after her operation was to run up 60 stairs.

"There was no treadmill in those days," says Margaret.

She knew Sully as a heart hospital and did not know until I told her that it was also a TB hospital.

(Heart and TB patients were strictly segregated.)

After her marriage she asked the doctors if she could have a family.

While Dr Davies in Sully said yes, the doctor she consulted near her home on the south coast advised against it, and sent a letter to Dr Davies explaining why. Margaret still has copies of those letters.

Throughout her life, Margaret has had to attend regular check-ups for her heart, and she enjoyed a normal life until nearly ten years ago, when her health deteriorated and she ended up in a wheelchair.

But a pioneering breakthrough came in 2009 when Margaret was approached by Victor Tsang, a world class cardiac surgeon undertaking risky repair of neonatal heart problems at Great Ormond Street hospital, London if she would be prepared, as the first adult in the UK, to undergo a groundbreaking operation.

"Well, I felt I had nothing to lose," she said. "It turned out to be a miracle. Within weeks I was walking again."

Today, she enjoys good health and loves taking long walks on the beach in Jersey with her husband of forty years.

Bernie Watts from Ontario, Canada: Seeking family history

"My father was in the Royal Welsh Fusiliers at the time.

All I know is that he had been very ill, as you can see his colleagues (see photo) were both servicemen, so I wonder if it served as a military hospital at one time.

My father was born in Bridgend in Glamorganshire and he joined the Army, serving time in Gibraltar, Shanghai, Hong Kong, Belgium and France. Sometime after the war he was transferred to the School of Combined Operations located in Barnstaple and it was around this time that he became sick. He'd married my mum in 1942; she lived in Hoylake on the Wirral, where he had been stationed during the earlier part

Bill Watts, centre, in Sully. Photo courtesy of Bernie Watts

of the war and where I grew up.

I have no information on Sully Hospital, apart from knowing that he was very ill and my mother went down to see him and for her to leave the children would have been significant.

Peggy Horton - patient

Peggy had her left lung removed and was sent home to live in a wooden shed, or chalet, in her parents' garden in Shirenewton, near Chepstow. (This was not unusual in those days.)

Her daughter, Ann Farmer explains: "The shed was provided by the Monmouthshire health authority. It was lined with fibreglass then another inner lining of wood. There was a paraffin heater, a bed and a chair. She lived in it for 18 months.

In 1954 she was cleared of TB and she married my father."

Peggy Horton with shed in background

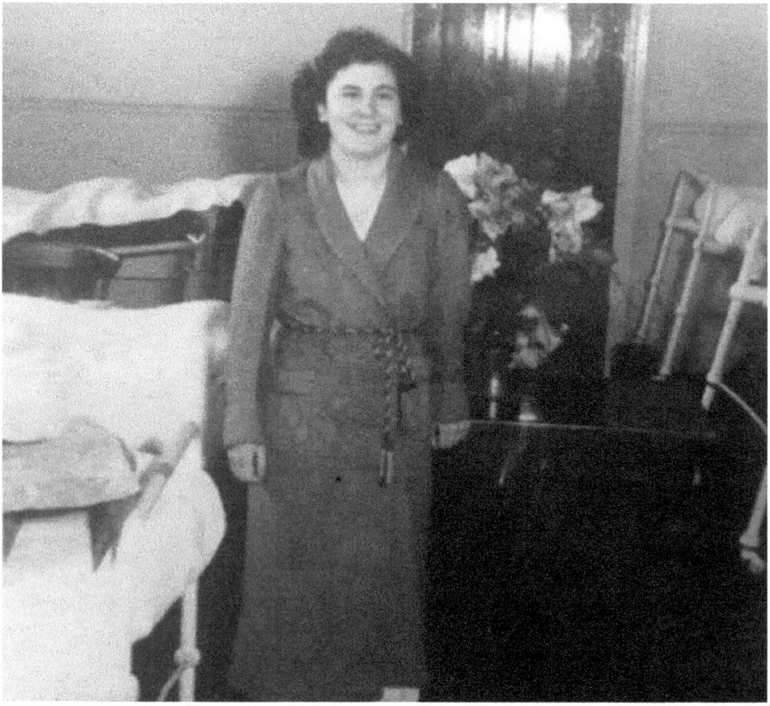

Peggy Horton inside Sully

"Looking back on her life, I now realise it must have been an incredible hard time for her, though she would regularly mention Christmas in Sully and joke about it."

STAFF
Pam Stephen – first hospital to do a "blue baby" operation

I worked as a clerk in the medical records office of Sully Hospital for six months in 1954.

"I had just returned from a year in France as an au pair, when I found myself on the same bus as Pat Edwards, who worked at Sully and she asked me what I was doing at that time. So it was that I found myself working with her in Medical Records at Sully Hospital, where she was the senior secretary to the Medical Superintendent, Dr Foreman – affectionately known as Father Foreman.

Some six weeks later I developed infective hepatitis (having had a clear Mantoux test three weeks previously) and was off work for six weeks. I later learnt that two of the theatres had been closed because of the virus - suggesting that the needles used for my test had not been thoroughly cleaned! Anyway, I returned to work.

Pat and I used to sing together a lot, which caused much amusement when overheard.

I remember the hospital as a very happy and caring place with lovely views and friendly staff. (I also remember that if I missed the bus in the morning, I had to get on my bike and pedal like mad to get there on time!)

Sully hit the news when it was the first hospital in the country to do a 'blue baby' heart operation: it was really a general thoracic hospital and very much up-to-date at that time. The Medical Superintendent, Dr Foreman, was a lovely man and well respected for the work he had done in a prisoner-of-war camp during an outbreak of typhoid.

His office adjoined medical records and he was on friendly terms with all the staff.

The diminishing role of Sully hospital began some 2-4 years later, when mass x-ray examinations picked up TB in its early stages, and hospitalisation was no longer needed.

STAFF STORIES

Pam Foreman, widow of Dr Bill Foreman, the hospital Superintendent at Sully offers some of her memories of Sully.

She recalls that surgeons practiced open-heart surgery on sheep, and afterwards sent them to one of the single wards kept for post-operative care in order to simulate as closely as possible the procedure intended for humans.

Such was the dedication of the surgeons and doctors that she remembers the wife of one surgeon saying that if she were a sheep she would see more of her husband.

Another practice amongst those early pioneers of open-heart surgery was the procedure of lowering the body temperature to allow heart surgery to take place. This involved wrapping the patient in blankets then lowering him into a bath full of ice.

This gave the surgeons a six-minute window of opportunity

Dr Len West and Dr Bill Foreman

to work on the heart.

Following the post-war period, there were great medical advances made for the treatment of TB, heralded by the discovery of streptomycin.

Once she heard her husband discussing alternative drug regimes with another doctor: "If X doesn't work let's try Y…" then he added: "If this works then we could be doing ourselves out of a job."

His prediction proved correct. For the new drug regime revolutionized the treatment of TB, which in turn led to surgeons retraining in heart surgery.

Even today former staff still speak with fondness of those far off days and the great family atmosphere engendered by Sully, then at its height as a great model-hospital.

Some of that is due to the family atmosphere generated by Dr Bill Foreman, the unassuming hospital superintendent, from New Zealand, and helped by another Antipodean Dr Len West, from Australia.

Certainly Sully encouraged close contacts with doctors from Third World countries and many gained their qualifications in thoracic medicine there.

Sunday lunch at the Foremans' for the foreign doctors was an established social event.

"Many had left their families behind and we offered them a bit of normality. They would play afterwards with our six children."

On Christmas Day, the Foreman children had to make sure all their presents were opened before 11 o'clock, because Dr Foreman had to go and carve the turkey for the patients.

On his return at three o'clock, the Foreman family could then enjoy their own Christmas dinner.

Aware of the isolation of Sully Hospital from the rest of the community, he recognized the need to introduce recreational facilities for the staff.

Through his foresight, energy and contacts with local charities, Sully Hospital got both a swimming pool and tennis courts for staff, and radio and telephones in the wards for the patients.

Daughter Jane Foreman said:

"We feel very attached to Sully. It was a wonderful place. Anna, my sister and GP working in South Wales, still meets former patients who speak so well of it and the staff and the

Dr Len West and Dr Bill Foreman with the medical team

atmosphere there.

I remember Dad being very keen to get a swimming pool for staff. He was aware that the hospital was out in the sticks and that it needed fun, and of course, being from New Zealand he loved water.

As children, we often had to wait in Sully while Dad finished work. The lovely telephone receptionist would let us sit with her and watch her handling the switchboard with its red tubes and plugs which fascinated us."

Sully became a victim of post-war hospital rationalisation, something that was of great sadness to him.

In New Zealand, he is still regarded as one of the most famous NZ expats in the UK.

Obituary

Dr Bill Foreman, born 1913, died 1976

"A New Zealander by birth, he was known to all as Bill after the first day of the month when bills arrived though his real name was Harold Mason.

Born on 1 December 1913 Bill Foreman was educated at Takapuna Grammar School and Otago University where he won rugby blue for the New Zealand universities.

After house appointments in Auckland he enlisted in the New Zealand Medical Corps and was taken prisoner in Greece while remaining with those wounded who were too ill to be evacuated.

He volunteered to be transferred to a camp where Russian prisoners were dying from typhus, and, in spite of contacting the disease himself, remained there for two years.

He worked tirelessly to alleviate the suffering of fellow British POWs in the Polish town of Cosel, and when the war ended he was awarded the MBE for his selfless work.

Throughout his life he was known for his great humanity and medical skill, often putting his own life in danger.

After the war he trained as a chest physician at the Brompton Hospital. He passed the MRCP in 1947 and was appointed physician superintendent of Sully Hospital in 1951.

There he was able to guide a team of physicians and surgeons in the control and cure of tuberculosis and then to develop a modern cardiothoracic unit while at the same time ensuring that his own humanity was reflected in the running of the hospital.

He knew all the staff personally and introduced many amenities that made life pleasant for them, and easier for the patients and their relatives.

In his later years it was a matter of great sorrow to him to see the hospital gradually broken up, and he continued to the last to fight for what he knew was best for his patients.

Bill was a man of great modesty. He never spoke of his past career, but his eminence in his specialty was recognized by his election as president of the Thoracic Society in 1972.

His knowledge of chest medicine, together with his common sense and sympathy, made him an outstanding colleague, but it is as a loyal and kind friend that he will be mourned by so many.

He bore his final illness with great courage, support by a strong Christian faith and by his family, to whom he was devoted. Dr Foreman is survived by his wife and six children."

Another lifelong friend, Archie Cochrane, added:

"I was privileged to know Bill Foreman for many years. We met first in London in 1940 on a course for Army medical officers."

We met again as prisoners-of-war in Salonika in 1941, and I was close to him and his family in South Wales for a long time.

Throughout this long and varied period, his cheerfulness and kindliness meant much to me, as to many others. He was, I think, the kindest man I have ever known."

(British Medical Journal, 29 May 1976 - Obituary Notices - H.M.Foreman MBE, MB, CHB, FRCP)

1960s

STAFF STORIES

Hugh Thorp - trained in Sully - Professor in Canada

I started my career as a nurse in Sully. I was an SRN at Sully from March 1964 until October 1967, and I worked in the Operating Theatres for my whole time there.

My principal reasons for working at Sully were that I already possessed a Post Graduate Certificate in O.R. Nursing and I wished to obtain my BTA. I was provided with a Council House on Barry Island (103 Phyllis Street), and with the low pay for nurses, this was a most important consideration in the 1960's.

I look back on my time at the hospital with fond remembrance. The Staff and the surgeons were first class and the work rewarding, particularly the cardio-vascular surgery which was often on newborn infants.

My family and I emigrated to Canada in 1967, and both my wife and I enjoyed rewarding careers in Health Care: she as a Supervisor of an Intensive Care at a major Teaching Hospital, and I as an RN, Educator, Hospital Administrator and University Professor.

The surgeons, Harley, Thomas and Rosser were all fine men with great skill. What comes through in all the correspondence I have received from ex staff at Sully is how much they valued their time there and how much they enjoyed working there too.

Steve Dorkings, Biomedical scientist - terrific camaraderie

My father was a patient at Sully in the early 60's.

I was about 9 years old and rarely allowed in to visit him (over 13's only). Despite serious illness over many months he still recounts happy times as a patient, including coaxing the seagulls into the ward from the balcony, much to sisters annoyance!

I started my career as a Junior Medical Laboratory Technician in Pathology, training to diagnose disease by laboratory methods at Sully Hospital. (The profession is now known as Biomedical Scientists.)

The Pathology department was then quite small, unlike the modern automated laboratories of today.

I was there from 1968 to 1972. I was taught everything from collecting blood on the wards for Haematology, to diagnosing TB from sputum examination. There were several trainees, pathology then just on the verge of great breakthroughs, nothing was automated, and I made very good friends.

I met and married my wife there, she was a junior nurse who later went onto be involved in ECG.

It was a great place to work, with the staff all knowing each other by first names from the coal boiler stoker "Ginger" to the hospital superintendent Dr "Bill" Foreman.

I was there when heart valve replacement and perfusion was being pioneered.

When on call for Biochemistry, I had to monitor the Na, K and blood gases of such patients from table to ITU, sometimes on the hour every hour, all afternoon and night. In Haematology we had to perform prothrombin and clotting times and cross-match blood. In those days cross-matching 20 pints of blood for an open heart patient wasn't a bad day!

Despite individual patients' sad fortunes, it was a great place to work and the staff had a terrific camaraderie and genuinely cared for the patients.

Sully put me on a career, which I pursued across Wales, Scotland and England, contributing to many pathology laboratories in the NHS. I have just retired after 42 years as a biomedical scientist, specialising in medical microbiology, and can honestly say the years spent at Sully were the best years of my career and equipped me with a passion for my subject, the NHS, its staff and most importantly, the patient. I learnt much more than just the science. Thank you Sully Hospital.

Steve Dorkings CSi, FIBMS, Cert. NHS Man.

(N.B. Before the introduction of laboratories guinea pigs were used to test if patients were positive or negative. If the guinea pigs lived you knew you were cured, or at least the disease was no longer in an infectious form.)

PATIENTS' STORIES

Stephen Parry - Most children died

Stephen, aged ten, was one of the first to undergo pioneering heart surgery in 1964.

I remember the long trek to the hospital with my mother from my home in Cwmbran, which involved about three buses as we didn't have a car. And the long walk past a plastics or chemical factory which we had to take when we missed the bus that dropped us off outside the hospital. I can still smell that factory now.

At the time I didn't understand how seriously ill I was or indeed how ill the other children on the ward were that became my friends. It wasn't until many years later that I was told that most of them had died either in hospital or soon after discharge.

Of course heart surgery was very much in its infancy at the time, and I was something of a pioneer, I suppose. My sister went on to become a nurse and discovered some time later that I was one of the first patients to use the heart lung machine.

My parents stayed in the hospital accommodation when I had the operation. It was in June 1964 (I can't remember the exact date), and I remember coming round after the operation in the post op room overlooking the sea. It was a moment I will never forget. It was a beautiful summer morning and the sun was dancing on the water. There were yachts as well I recall. My parents were at my side and my mother burst into tears on seeing the aftermath of the surgery.

I suppose it couldn't have been a pretty sight with stitches and draining tubes coming out of my body. The surgeon Mr. Harley told me later I had 63 stitches.

Jenny Hicks - Still dream of the place

I was 12 years old in 1962 when I was diagnosed with non cystic fibrosis and a rare skin disease called Steven-Johnson syndrome.

The latter condition was brought on as a six year old when I had a severe reaction to antibiotics.

The doctors told me I would never work or have children. I defied them. I did both.

Despite over 50 years of ill health and constant pain she is remarkably cheerful. She lives in Cowbridge.

I have very fond memories of Sully and I still dream of the place.

David Roberts - Regular trips to the Sully Arms

I remember my mother's shame about me having TB and the house being fumigated and people in the village thinking I had been neglected, despite being the most well-fed and cared-for lad in the village.

I dreaded what I was about to experience at Sully when I was admitted as a 19 year old with a shadow on the lung.

But I was to experience six excellent months there.

After a few days, the "hotel" experience kicked in once I had come to terms with the prospects of 6 months confinement.

Quickly, "confinement" became a relative term and, along with two other new friends, we trekked regularly along the rocks to enjoy a few pints at the Sully Arms.

We always used the bar area, presuming any staff from the hospital would more likely choose the lounge.

Other regular afternoon trips were undertaken to Barry High Street and the Docks. On one occasion we were driven to make a quick exit from a shop in the High Street on encountering the "battle axe" Sister England. (The same Sister that banned me using a short dressing gown on the basis of it being a smoking jacket.)

All in all, it was a wonderful experience and a productive one too. The Friends of Sully funded a Book Keeping correspondence course for me, which later proved invaluable in business, and an arrangement was made for me to work in the records department on a part time basis. (Try that today under the Data Protection Act!

I remember being allowed to work with two other patients on the hospital radio service (D.J.ing with huge BBC-like equipment) down in the basement, next to redundant x-ray machines destined for the Third World.

The basement was also the venue for the hospital staff giving the patients a special show before Xmas (I remember their rendition of "Just one more cigarette" vividly).

I also remember befriending a number of sheep held in the field adjoining the hospital whose purpose was for scientific research.

1970s

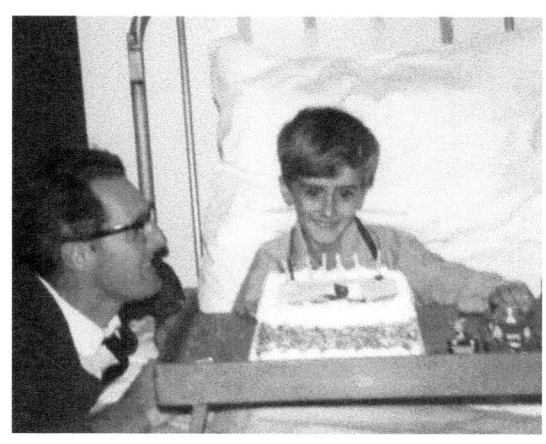

PATIENTS' STORIES

Warren Lewis – I still have my poster from Sully

Warren Lewis was born in 1964 with Fallots Tetralogy, a congenital heart defect.

In 1971 at the age of seven years, he had an operation in Sully to correct it.

"I was on Morgannwg ward and I still have the present, a poster of Donald Duck, which all the staff signed."

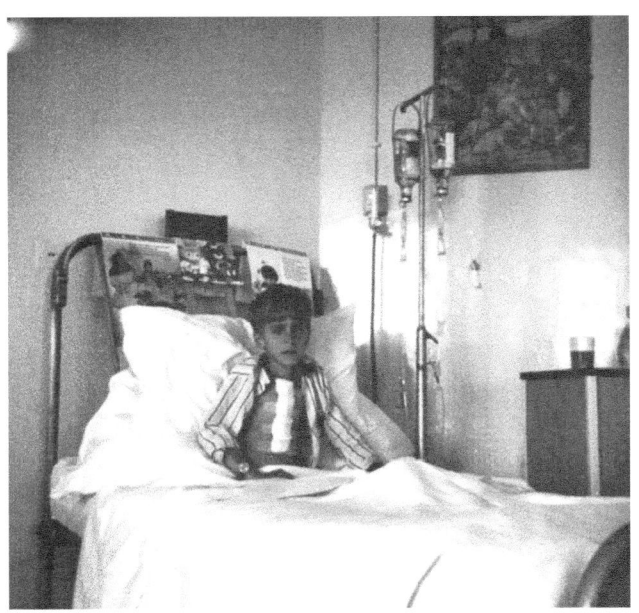

Warren all wired up after his operation

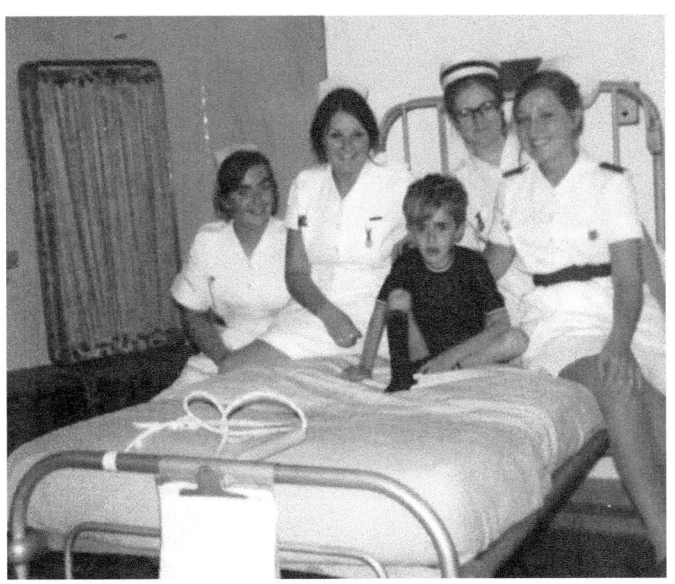

Warren with the nurses: "They were lovely to me."

Warren (front) with other children in Sully.

Ceri Williams (nee Pritchard) - Happy Days

Every time Ceri Williams flies out of Cardiff airport she passes over Sully Hospital, looks down and says to herself:

"Happy days!"

For Ceri was there as a hole-in-the-heart child patient there in the early 1970s.

She talks of her time at Sully with fond memories.

"I was very friendly with a boy called Kevin and we would run outside on to the beach in our pyjamas to collect crabs from the rock pools then we would carry them back and put them in the bath. The nurses would go spare.

Sometimes they could not find us to give us our treatment, or procedures, because we were out on the beach."

Medicine moved on and at 24 years of age Ceri elected to have hole-in-the-heart surgery at Brompton Hospital London.

"This was very successful and it changed my life."

Today she lives in Abercynon, between Merthyr and Cardiff, part of a close-knit family and community.

"I asked about having children and I was advised against it. Now it's too late," she says.

"But I am happy, I have all my family and friends around me. I have always lived in the valleys. I see no reason to move".

Howard Richards: Only chance of survival

"I was one of the first children to have a heart operation using the new heart-lung machine, and I was ten years of age at the time.

My mother kept telling the doctors that there was something wrong with me and eventually a surgeon confirmed it. I had a heart murmur."

Now in his early 60's and recently retired, he still has his hospital appointment book.

His parents were told that he would be dead by the time he was thirteen or fourteen and the only chance he had of survival, and it was a slender one, was to risk having this new heart operation.

"Well, they were faced with this dreadful decision," said Howard."They took the chance. And I survived."

Howard went on to lead a very healthy life.

STAFF

Vivienne Griffin – Feeding the babies

"We used to sit feeding the babies in the dark January mornings watching the sun come up over the sea," said Nurse Vivienne Griffin, who did part of her pediatric training in Sully Hospital.

We used to prepare the babies' bottles in Black Beard's cupboard (I don't know why it was called that).

Sometimes, when we were feeding the babies, the cardiologist, Mr. Davies would say: "Right girls, I've got twenty minutes, you can ask me anything you want."

He would sit down and draw diagrams of the heart and explain any abnormalities. We had a wonderful time there."

Janet Phillip – living in Australia

Staff nurse Janet Phillip worked in Sully during the 1970s. She remembers it as a very happy period of her life and it was there that she met and married Dr Keith Wong. Later they moved

Staff Janet Phillip

to New Zealand.

Tragically he died of cancer while only 45 years of age and Janet brought his ashes back to Sully where they are scattered in the grounds within view of his old cardiac unit. "I was 28 in the first photo taken in the National Heart Hospital, London where I worked in the pediatric cardiac unit and I am 59 in the second photo – taken in Australia where I live now.

"It must be the must be the good Welsh genes!!"

Janet says: "I trained as a nurse at Llandough Hospital and visited Sully Hospital during my training. I knew that I wanted to work there so when I qualified in 1974, after my obligatory 6 months as a junior staff nurse at Llandough, I applied for a position at Sully.

"I started there on Powys Ward. the thoracic medical ward... 48 beds. This is where I met Dr. Foreman. He was a lovely man. I remember him telling me that he came from Takapuna. It meant very little to me at the time but later on I met and married a New Zealand cardiology registrar, Dr Keith Wong who came to Sully.

He was registrar to Dr Davies from 1976-78.

Later we went to live in New Zealand, and I visited Takapuna and thought of Dr. Foreman.

I was asked to transfer to the cardiology ward Morgannwg as a senior staff nurse and there I spent some of the happiest years of my nursing career. There was an enormous camaraderie amongst the staff. Dr Davies was the senior cardiologist and he was an amazing clinician and a modest and charming man.

I lived in the nurses' home while I worked at Sully. I was always very aware how fortunate I was to live somewhere where I woke up to the sound of the sea and the birds every morning. The ward patients also had this. What a wonderful place.

I left Sully in 1978 and moved to London and then to New Zealand. My husband became a consultant cardiologist in Christchurch. NZ.

Sadly, at the early age of 45, he died after a short and sharp battle with cancer. I met him at Sully and completed the circle by bringing his ashes back to scatter in the grounds of Sully Hospital, within view of the old cardiac catheter suite where he spent so much of his time.

Janet in Australia

Sully Hospital will always remain in my memories.

It was indeed a very happy hospital. Everyone knew everyone (and what they were up to!).

In 2007 Janet moved to Kalgoorlie, western Australia where she now lives with her second husband who works as an anaesthetist, and she has retired from nursing.

Meanwhile her children still live in the UK and her daughter resides in Barry.

Janet says: "I return regularly to visit them."

Adrian Pike- international reputation for heart surgery

I worked in Sully during the early 1970s and trained as a heart-lung bypass technician and so my responsibilities were to maintain the patients' blood flow, blood pressure and other physiological parameters while the surgeons operated on the patients.

This sometimes involved lowering the patient's body temperature to allow more time for open-heart surgery. The patients were all ages, from babies suffering from congenital heart disease, to older patients with heart valve or lung problems.

Sully Hospital had an international reputation for cardiothoracic surgery and was recognized as a premier institution.

Of course, the experience gained by the staff was some of the best in the world as some of the surgical procedures were the most innovative and some had actually been developed there.

Although these were major operations it was always wonderful to see these patients walking around and being discharged from the hospital.

I remember some of the doctors and surgeons there. Dr. Horton was the head of our team that included David Chapman and Nigel Salih. Dr. Foreman (the hospital superintendent), and some of the surgeons were Mr. Harley, Mr. Dilwyn Thomas, Mr. Rees, and Mr. Shah. Dr. L. G. Davies, who was director of the Cardiac Catheter Lab and all his wonderful staff. And, of course, all the dedicated theatre nurses including Mr. Jenkins the theatre supervisor.

I have such good memories of the time I worked there. Even though they were long days working in the theatres and there were days when I don't remember seeing the sunrise or sunset.

I do remember that the staff used to put on an excellent Christmas pantomime for all the patients that was always very funny and entertaining. This was always held in the main dining room.

After leaving Sully I worked at the Tenovus Institute for Cancer Research for many years. Then I joined the Medical School in Denver where I did research for the last 30 years.

Adrian Pike is now retired and living in Denver, Colorado.

1980s

STAFF

Steve Parker - Party time in the nurses' home.

Steve worked as a maintenance carpenter in Sully from 1983 to 1989.

I was only 21 years of age when I started there and moved from my parents home into the Nurses' Home. My room was 131, on the first floor of the Nurses Home, next to the lift (East Wing) and opposite the communal toilets with a view of the kitchens.

It was very tiny. My initial thoughts were: "What have I done!"

After unpacking on my first evening, I sat in my chair and left the door wide open.

I had a great view of the toilets. I just sat there and drank a few tins of beer.

After two hours there were sounds of laughter and a young girl appeared in the doorway dressed in her nightclothes.

She said: "Hello, are you new? Do you want to join us in the kitchen?

We're having a séance."

Well, I had never been to a séance before but I thought I would give it a try.

Well, there were about six or so students all sat around a coffee table, all in their night dresses and a couple of empty bottles of wine and me.

We were unable to contact the dead but it did change my mind about staying.

Sian Phillips was the Warden. She lived on the first floor at the very end of the West wing. She left in 1986 and the new warden Gloria Rowe, was married and did not live in the nurses' home.

Eventually the porters got fed up of letting locked-out students back into their rooms, and I became unofficially the deputy warden as I had a set of master keys (part of my job).

Anyway, most of the time I was out with the students.

There were lots of parties in the nurses' home and only a few ever got out of hand with the warden having to put a stop to it.

Another regular event was the ritual walk to the Sully Inn on a Thursday night for a few beers and to listen to a singer.

In the summer we had beach parties with a BBQ.

Most of the students did not take to the social club in the grounds because it was a bit run down and was mostly frequented by employees of the hospital and locals.

They preferred to go to the students union in Cardiff or into Cardiff itself.

Life in the nurses' home was not all fun, and at times it got very quiet, especially in the summer holidays when there would only be about 6 of us in the home.

There would be some doctors, mainly from Africa or Asia attending residential courses. I remember a Dr Ali, a nice chap from Africa who was trying to get the cooker to work and he asked me to help.

He was using a lighter but could not understand why it was not lighting. The cooker was electric.

Then there was the time when another foreign doctor left his underwear boiling in a large saucepan in the kitchen.

He forgot about it.

The fire alarm went off, which it did from time to time, and we ignored it.

Suddenly there was smoke in the corridors and we found what remained of his clothes glowing and smouldering in the pan.

As usual the fire brigade turned up and there were half a dozen fire fighters crammed in the kitchen. We never did find out which doctor did it.

Whilst I was staying at the nurses' home I did two parachute jumps for charity to raise money for a new special bed, and I took part in a charity football match played at the BP social club in Sully, where all the hospital staff dressed up as nurses, including myself.

I think I gave a few people a bit of a shock for I rode through Sully on my motorbike in a size 12 staff nurses uniform, well endowed of course, complete with fishnet stockings.

Christmas at Sully was mixed for me: the atmosphere in the hospital itself was great with parties going on here and there, some even had small quantities of alcohol, and of course the staff Christmas dinner was a fine meal.

However, the nurses' home was once again quiet, although I worked in between Christmas and the New Year more often than not.

It was December 6th 1988, when I was asked to help a nurse who had finished her shift and was unable to start her scooter.

I tried everything that I could think of but it was not having any of it.

Just as I was putting away my tools a voice from above said, "Steve do you want to come to a party?"

"I am still in my working clothes," I said.

"Come as you are."

To this day I'm not sure who invited me, but when I walked into the first floor kitchen, a party was trying to get going, mostly girls and just a few lads.

This short blonde student chatted me up. Seven and a half years later we were married, and still are. My wife said that there was not much competition so she made a move first before anyone else did."

They got married in 1995 and live five miles from Craig-y-nos Castle in the Swansea Valley.

Wayne Spencer - great community spirit.

I worked as an apprentice electrician in Sully from October 1983 to January 1985.

I remember arriving there after being based at Llandough hospital and thinking 'Oh my God! Where have they sent me!'

It seemed miles from my home in Church Village (in reality only about 20 miles!).

I have worked at few places before or since with quite the community spirit of Sully Hospital.

Yes, there were arguments amongst the electricians, the fitters and the engineers in charge, but the hospital as a whole had a unique atmosphere.

There was very much a reciprocal help-each-other-out attitude that is definitely missing from the NHS today. I remember several times going into the canteen after a long afternoon shift and asking what was for dinner to be asked, "What would you like?"

I spent four months of my time at Sully installing new lighting and power cables in the underground ducts running between the boiler house (now gone it seems from the new development pictures) and the main hospital. I'm sure I never saw daylight for at least a week at a time! I wonder if the service ducts still run under the old hospital now it is flats. They were large enough to walk through in places. The boiler house and estates buildings were located to the left of the hospital as you look up the road, just near to the "sheep labs".

1990s

PATIENT'S STORY

Tony Blackwell - Hot meals delivered from Bristol

I was a patient in Sully in the late 90s when it was a psychiatric hospital.

My psychiatrist at the time felt that I needed a break in a safe environment and that's how I came to be sent to Sully.

I suffer from chronic clinical depression and haven't been able to work for the last fifteen years. It's with me on a daily basis, but like any other disability, one learns to live with it.

I wasn't really getting any treatment at the time apart from somewhat rudimentary occupational therapy.

I had previously had a couple of spells in Whitchurch Hospital in Cardiff.

But Sully, in many ways felt like a more relaxed environment. I think this had a lot to do with the relatively small amount of patients and, of course, the beautiful surroundings. I would often walk along the cliffs there and down to Sully Island and

Cosmeston Lakes.

One day a female ward manager was attacked by a newly arrived patient and one of the other patients came to her rescue.

We never saw her again and the staff got very strict after that with patient supervision.

Sully also seemed to be a place where recovering alcoholics were sent. Perhaps this was due to the remoteness of the hospital. I do know that some patients managed to get alcohol smuggled in and hid it in the grounds.

I was there for three months and the place was sadly in some disrepair.

I seem to remember that there was pretty much just the one ward open at the time – this included a special side ward for pregnant and young mothers with psychiatric problems.

It seemed to me the building was being used to store a lot of NHS records. I can clearly remember a couple of us exploring another floor and finding boxes and boxes of dental records, for example.

Due to cutbacks hot meals were no longer prepared on the premises. They came by van from Bristol every day, a distance of some 30 miles.

Sometimes the van got held up and we had our food very late. We would be starving.

I have fond memories of Sully – more so than the time I spent at Whitchurch Hospital where I received ECT.

It was such a beautiful building and it was easy to see that at one time it would have been spectacular.

Another patient and myself used to get to the dining room early for breakfast, as there were glorious sunrises visible from that room.

Sully closed as a hospital in 2001.

Postscript

Sully, the pioneering "model hospital" for the treatment of TB, is now a footnote in Welsh medical history.

Today this Art Deco building has been re-named Hayes Point - a stunning block of exclusive apartments for aspirational young people from Cardiff.